ENVIRONMENTAL HAZARDS
Human and Policy Dimensions

T0361132

ENVIRONMENTAL HAZARDS: Human and Policy Dimensions (EHAZ) is an innovative, interdisciplinary and international research journal addressing the human and policy dimensions of hazards.

The journal addresses the full range of hazardous events from extreme geological, hydrological atmospheric and biological events such as earthquakes, floods, storms and epidemics to technological failures and malfunctions such as industrial explosions, fires and toxic material releases. EHAZ is the source of the new ideas in hazards and risk research.

With a genuinely international perspective, this journal highlights issues of human exposure, vulnerability, awareness, response and risk. The role of hazards in development, and issues of efficiency, social justice and sustainability are also explored in the journal.

Well known conventional hazards receive extensive coverage but submissions about new forms of hazard, emerging risk management institutions and restructuring of ideas about hazards – including their role in human affairs – are particularly welcome.

Reinvigorating the debate about how we define, understand and manage hazards, the journal is interdisciplinary in scope and open to contributions by specialists from a wide range of fields who are interested in the effects of hazards events on people, property and societies.

Editor

Prof Edmund Penning-Rowsell
Flood Hazard Research Centre
Middlesex University
UK
E-mail: Edmund@penningrowsell.com

Associate Editor

Prof John Handmer
Centre for Risk and Community Safety
RMIT University
Australia
E-mail: john.handmer@rmit.edu.au

Editorial Board

Mr Stephen Bender
Organization of American States (Retired)
USA

Dr Neil Britton
Asian Development Bank
The Philippines

Prof Ian Davis
Cranfield University
UK

Dr Kenneth Hewitt
Wilfrid Laurier University
Canada

Dr Allan Lavell
Latin American Social Science Faculty
Costa Rica

Prof Peter J. May
University of Washington
USA

Dr Burrell Montz
Binghamton University
USA

Dr Betty Hearn Morrow
Florida International University
USA

Prof Roger Pielke
Centre for Science and Technology Research
USA

Prof Boris Porfiriev
Russian Academy of Sciences
Russia

Dr John P. Tiefenbacher
Texas State University
USA

Dr Juha I. Uitto
United Nations Development Programme
USA

Dr Peter Walker
Tufts University
USA

Dr Ben Wisner
Oberlin College
USA

ENVIRONMENTAL HAZARDS
Human and Policy Dimensions

VOLUME 8 ISSUE 3 2009
SPECIAL ISSUE

Special issue: Climate change as environmental and economic hazard

First published by Earthscan in the UK and USA in 2009

For a full list of publications please contact:

Earthscan
2 Park Square, Milton Park, Abingdon, Oxfordshire OX14 4RN
Simultaneously published in the USA and Canada by Earthscan
711 Third Avenue, New York, NY 10017

First issued in paperback 2016

*Earthscan is an imprint of the Taylor & Francis Group,
an informa business*

Environmental Hazards 8(3) September 2009.

© 2009 Earthscan

ISSN: 1747-7891 (print), 1878-0059 (online)

ISBN 13: 978-1-138-97092-2 (pbk)
ISBN 13: 978-1-84971-089-3 (hbk)

Abstracting services which cover this title include
Elsevier Scopus and GeoRef

Environmental Hazards is published quarterly. Periodicals
Postage Paid at Rahway, NJ. US agent: Mercury
International, 365 Blair Road, Avenel, NJ 07001.
POSTMASTER: Address changes to ENVIRONMENTAL
HAZARDS, 365 Blair Road, Avenel, NJ 07001.

from Routledge

Climate change: A hazard or an opportunity?

Boris Porfiriev*

Guest Editor, Risk and Crisis Research Center at the Institute of Economics, Russian Academy of Sciences, Novocheriomushkinskaia, 42a, 117418 Moscow, Russia

Climate change is a serious environmental hazard that affects communities and economies worldwide. Many of the impacts of climate change are already in place with even more in number and severity expected in the future, seriously jeopardizing and compromising global economic development goals. Although the agents of the impact are diverse and involve significant fluctuations in the amount of precipitation, severity of the winds and rising sea levels, to name a few, rising temperatures are mentioned elsewhere in research literature and media as a major driver (and effect) of climate change and of global warming in particular.

Indeed, since the Industrial Revolution the mean surface temperature of Earth has increased by an average of 2°C with most of this change occurring in the past 30–40 years, and the rate of increase appears to be accelerating. The leaders of the major G8 economies at the July 2009 Summit in Italy declared their recognition of the broad scientific view that the increase in global average temperature above pre-industrial levels ought not to exceed 2°C. It was also acknowledged that meeting such a challenge requires a global response with all countries sharing the ambitious goal of achieving at least a 50 per cent reduction in total global 'greenhouse gas' CO_2 emissions by 2050, and recognizing the difference in implementation capacity between developed and developing countries. The former are expected to reduce emissions of greenhouse gases in aggregate by 80 per cent or more by 2050 compared to 1990 (or more recent years). Major emerging economies need to undertake quantifiable actions collectively to reduce emissions significantly below business-as-usual by a specified year (Major Economies Forum, 2009).

However, such joint and spectacular declarations cannot conceal two types of persisting discrepancy. One set of doubts and disagreements exists within the research community and concerns the major drivers of climate change. The mainstream, headed by the IPCC with a 'more than 90 per cent' confidence range, maintains that anthropogenic impact is key. Basing this crucial judgement on the consensus between some 2,500 experts involved in the IPCC process, the panel's leaders are supported by many top politicians including the UN General Secretary. Some past and present leaders in the USA and Europe imply such a consensus has been reached within the whole research community. However, opponents do exist. These opponents pinpoint the weaknesses of the climate models used by the IPCC. They argue that much evidence points to natural factors as a major driver of climate fluctuations in the long-term retrospective (measured in centuries rather than decades) and at least as an important agent of recent change.

The point here is not to step on the shaky soil of disputing who is more correct in physical terms – as I am not a climatologist it is not worth even trying this – but rather to emphasize the issue of degree of uncertainty which is paramount in political and economic respects. Indeed, following the mainstream interpretation of climate change, assuming the human contribution to this change amounts to as much as two-thirds of the total with the confidence range of this assessment reaching 0.91,[1] would produce an expectancy value of 60 per cent. However high and salient from an ecological perspective, such a value could hardly be perceived as a sufficient condition for the decision to give priority to the unequivocal investment of political and/or monetary capital in the reduction of human impact on climate. At least, within the framework of economic theory, mainstream or neoclassic economics would regard this value as complying much more with venture – or even speculation – rather than with 'normal' capital investment.

This adds to other predicaments of policy decision making, including consideration of the major risks and challenges to development and security other than climate

■ *E-mail: b_porfiriev@mail.ru

ENVIRONMENTAL HAZARDS 8 (2009) 167–170

doi:10.3763/ehaz.2009.0026 © 2009 Earthscan ISSN: 1747-7891 (print), 1878-0059 (online) www.earthscanjournals.com

change, in particular those associated with the current economic crisis. As a result, one more set of disputes and controversies persists within business and political communities concerning the most efficient policy strategy for coping with climate change implications for the environment, the economy and society as a whole. These involve cleavages between both the advocates and antagonists of 'greening' economic policy in specific nations and between nations, in particular the countries of Annex I and non-Annex I of the Kyoto Protocol. Within the latter, disagreements between the USA, EU and major emerging economies led by China proved to be most important to the development of international climate policy, including the success or failure of the forthcoming summit in Copenhagen in December 2009.

Reducing the political, social and economic implications of climate change and the risks associated with future climate policy requires concentration of efforts on two interrelated policy areas or directions. The first involves decreasing the degree of uncertainty about the above-mentioned implications of climate change and climate change itself. This calls for more investment of human and pecuniary resources in Earth science research – a unique source of data enrichment and knowledge bases as well as better understanding of the yet poorly or insufficiently recognized laws of nature that drive climate change. In turn, this should facilitate development of real scientific fundamentals of coping policy, devoid of current 'militaristic' conceptualization as revealed by the titles of international and national programme documents full of 'fight', 'combat' and other offensive and defensive operations 'against' climate change (for example, see UNDP, 2007). Whatever the disputes about the specific amount of natural variability input into global climate change, none of the IPCC scholars – let alone their opponents – doubt its conspicuous contribution; throughout its history mankind has accumulated too much experience of the consequences of 'conquering' or 'struggling against' nature. New research findings will bring more evidence and substantiation of genuine efficient climate policy which seriously considers and adapts to – rather than fights against – nature.

The second policy area or direction focuses on what is known as mainstreaming climate policy into the overall development strategy. This initially implies the conceptualization of the multiplicity and salience of major challenges to development and security, all of which require political and public awareness and economic resources for timely and efficient policy treatment. In particular – and of no less significance than climate change – natural and human-made hazards should be considered and contrasted against climate change and its implications. Such a comparison should involve weighing the full gamut of risks, costs and benefits of handling these hazards using a multi-criteria and systems approach towards the setting of policy priorities and resource sharing.

In addition to and developing from these conceptual issues, several implementation measures should be employed. At the microeconomic level these range from specific energy-saving and energy-efficient measures for reducing carbon emissions to comprehensive risk management systems built into the corporate management structures for handling all kinds of risks, from financial to environmental. At the macroeconomic level these include the state providing institutional support to businesses and households to help them cut down emissions, and integration of both climate change and disaster risk reduction policies into national and international development strategies. This should include the incorporation of 'green' or 'low-carbon' economy development programmes into national anti-hazard policy packages.

In relation to the latter, it is worth mentioning that 30 OECD member countries together with five candidates for accession (Chile, Estonia, Israel, Russia and Slovenia) and five Enhanced Engagement Partner countries (Brazil, China, India, Indonesia and South Africa) will implement the packages above worth more than US$2.3 trillion between 2008 and 2010. These are the largest global fiscal stimuli in history and at the same time could be considered 'the greatest opportunity ever had for "greening" national economies' (Gurria, 2009). Already the governments have allocated more than US$430 billion in fiscal stimulus to key climate change investment issues alone, or almost 16 per cent of the total amount of these packages. China and the USA, the major contributors to greenhouse gas emissions, lead the way in absolute terms of resources to be spent, while South Korea, the EU and France are at the top of the list in terms of the percentage of the total stimulus in relation to the sizes of the economies (81, 59 and 21 per cent, respectively). Key sectoral beneficiaries include rail transportation, water infrastructure, grid expansion including 'smart grid' development and improved building efficiency. Renewable energy has received limited support in present packages, except in the USA (Robins et al., 2009, pp. 2–3).

However, the most important aspect of the above commitments is that one should perceive them as but the first instalment of further efforts by governments to use 'green' growth as a master key lever for both economic recovery (inclusive of G20 recovery talks) and to strengthen the policy of reducing climate change hazards – including the Copenhagen climate negotiations – instead of using the excuse of the current economic recession to decelerate this policy. One could cite the Green Growth Declaration recently endorsed by OECD members and some non-member countries in evidence of this tendency.

The above illuminates the perspective that climate change is not only a hazard and a challenge but also a bifurcation point marking an opportunity to shift to a new sustainable development policy. The latter suggests thinking 'out of the box' and drifting away from mainstream climate and economic theories that constitute the basis of modern development. From a natural science perspective such a shift implies a new paradigm which considers climate change a phenomenon fraught with an increasing number and severity of abrupt fluctuations in environmental conditions, driven by natural variability and anthropogenic – primarily technological – factors with the specific contribution of each remaining uncertain.

From a social science (particularly economic) perspective, the characteristics above assume resource allocation marrying with a multi-hazard approach, on the one hand, with *in dubio mitius or* precautionary principle. This involves consideration of the 'long tail' and intergenerational modes of climate change impact and thus implies special monetary and/or insurance funds to cover respective costs and expected damage. On the other hand, looking at the principle of impact differentiation and considering the controversial effect of climate change on regions, communities and industries, it is clear that some people will lose in economic and life terms while others will benefit or gain from altering environmental conditions.

Finally, from a national and global policy perspective the new conceptualization of climate change and climate policy implies transition to matching mitigation and adaptation policies with the priority shifting towards adaptation policy. The latter in no way assumes depreciation of mitigation efforts to reduce CO_2 and other greenhouse gas emissions. It rather aims to improve existing climate policy, which is inefficient in two important ways.

First, one must seriously consider the salience of the responsible international and national agencies' issue of residual risk, i.e. climate change impact after the best mitigation measures possible have been implemented. As mentioned elsewhere in earlier research literature, even total suspension of current and future greenhouse gas emissions would not mean a resolution of the problem, given the remaining hazard precipitated by the huge amount of such gases accumulated in the past. Such an option is only pure theory.

Second, the significance of the natural variability component of climate change must be taken into account, underestimated or shadowed as it is now by the dominant anthropogenic theory of global warming. In-depth analysis of world disaster statistics proves that, if the recurrence of meteorological hazards is assumed to be constant, the damage inflicted by disaster agents would increase dramatically given the proportionate increase of the vulnerability of communities and industrial assets driven by accelerated urbanization and economic growth.

This special issue of *Environmental Hazards* was conceived as an attempt to focus the reader's attention on problems mentioned above that need more coverage and deeper investigation. The issue starts with discussion about the paradigm shift, signs of which are already visible. However, much still needs to be done in order to develop a comprehensive framework embedding the improved climate policy into a sustainable development strategy. For such a framework, the paper by a group of scholars from Yale and Wesleyan Universities in the USA suggests a holistic and dynamic systems approach, focusing on socio-ecological resilience as a means of tackling the inherent uncertainty associated with climate change and hazard events and the primary objectives for adaptation and risk reduction. Two specific mechanisms for transformative change in these fields involve: iterative risk management as a primary instrument for adaptive decision making; and institutional changes – particularly the establishment of 'boundary organizations' – to increase the transfer of knowledge between science, policy and practice.

The next pair of contributions address the risk reduction or mitigation issue. Pielke's paper concerns predicaments of forecasting hazards associated with climate change and the damage it produces. In particular, it considers the incremental efficiency of one- to five-year predictions of US hurricane landfalls and damages, added to a baseline expectation derived from the long-term climatological record. It is argued that the large diversity of available predictions means that some predictions will improve upon climatology, but for decades if not longer it will be impossible to know whether the improvement was due to chance or actual forecasting skill. An important recommendation for decision makers here is to use climatology as a baseline expectation and clearly to identify hedges away from this baseline, in order clearly to distinguish between empirical and non-empirical substantiations of climate risk assessment.

The paper by Fankhauser, Kennedy and Skea tackles mitigation from a different – an institutional – perspective, using the UK 2008 Climate Change Act as a case study. This normative document, the first of its kind in the world, legally binds the national level greenhouse emissions to a tough target for 2050: at least 80 per cent, relative to 1990. It also establishes a new institutional architecture to ensure this long-term objective is achieved, including a series of statutory five-year carbon budgets. The first three of these (for the years 2008–2022) were set in spring 2009 and assume an emissions cut of 34 per cent. Recommending the targets and overseeing compliance with them is a new independent body, the Committee on Climate Change. This paper summarizes the 2008 inaugural report published by the Committee and explains the analytical basis behind its recommendations.

Finally, the last two contributions contemplate the issue of adaptation to climate change and its implications on communities and the economy, also in two respects. The paper by Botzen and van den Bergh concerns managing disasters, the bulk of which have been provoked by meteorological agents. It stresses a high probability of the augmentation of disaster damage trends in the future due to a combination of climate and socio-economic change impact. This requires a more sophisticated disaster risk management policy based on the concept of community resilience, comprising a package of measures focused on disaster risk prevention, damage mitigation and arrangements for efficient risk sharing. Especially emphasized is the salient role of financial systems and tools such as insurance in the adaptation to climate change aimed at reducing the damage and facilitating recovery from meteorological disasters.

Olsson's paper analyses the issue of adaptation to climate change from a different perspective, namely a crisis management framework with a particular emphasis on crisis communication. Crises associated with or amplified by climate change impact involve a broad range of economic, environmental and social issues that require specific and comprehensive policies capable of efficiently addressing different groups of actors. Building upon earlier research findings on political crisis communication, the author contemplates these actors' framing strategies in connection with the crises above and the way these are affected by the media, using the case study of the drought in the Murray–Darling Basin in Australia and its coverage in the local press.

The contributors to this special issue – and the Guest Editor – hope that contemplation of the points above will add a valuable grain to the 'goldfield' of earlier findings in climate change research. They might just catalyse a new turn of the discussion spiral on the 'hazard–opportunity' duality of this new global challenge.

Note

1. Both of these assumptions fully comply with the IPCC notion of anthropogenic factor being 'very likely' (i.e. with confidence rate over 90 per cent) to be the 'major cause' of climate change.

References

Gurria, A., 2009. From grim to green: towards a low-carbon future. Remarks delivered by the OECD General Secretary at the International Economic Forum of the Americas (Conference of Montreal), 9 June. Montreal, Canada. www.oecd.org/document/58/0,3343, en_2649_34487_43031674_1_1_1_1,00.html.

Major Economies Forum, 2009. *Declaration of the Major Economies Forum on Energy and Climate*, 8–10 July. l'Aquila, Italy. www.g8italia2009.it/static/G8_Allegato/ MEF_Declarationl.pdf.

Robins, N., Clover, R. and Singh, C., 2009. *Climate for Recovery: The Color of Stimulus Goes Green*. HSBC Global Research, London.

UNDP, 2007. *Human Development Report 2007/2008. Fighting Climate Change: Human Solidarity in a Divided World*. UNDP, New York.

research article

ENVIRONMENTAL
HAZARDS
Human and Policy Dimensions

Strengthening socio-ecological resilience through disaster risk reduction and climate change adaptation: Identifying gaps in an uncertain world

WILLIAM M. COLLIER[1,*], KASEY R. JACOBS[1], ALARK SAXENA[1], JULIANNE BAKER-GALLEGOS[1], MATTHEW CARROLL[1] AND GARY W. YOHE[2]

[1]School of Forestry and Environmental Studies, Yale University, 195 Prospect Street, New Haven, CT 06511, USA
[2]Department of Economics, Wesleyan University, 238 Church Street, Middletown, CT 06459, USA

Global environmental change and climate change are rapidly altering the world's socio-ecological systems and affecting human populations at multiple scales. Important manifestations of these changes are hazard and disaster events. The emerging fields of climate change adaptation and disaster risk reduction provide significant opportunities to avoid and/or reduce many of the negative consequences associated with such events. Reviewing current attempts to link these two fields, we suggest an urgent need for a holistic and dynamic systems approach, focusing on socio-ecological resilience as a primary objective for adaptation and risk reduction. Furthermore, we propose two mechanisms for transformative change in these fields: (1) the use of iterative risk management as a primary instrument for adaptive decision making, and (2) the establishment of 'boundary organizations' and institutional changes that increase the transfer of knowledge between not only science and policy, but also science, policy and practice. There is immediate demand for participatory scholarly research to address the needs and concerns of practitioners on the ground. As a framework for these concepts, we see a dynamic systems approach to socio-ecological resilience as a means to deal with the inherent uncertainty associated with climate change and hazard events.

Keywords: adaptive management; boundary organizations; dynamic systems theory; knowledge networks; uncertainty; vulnerability

1. Introduction

Global environmental change is occurring at rates unprecedented in human history, challenging the resilience and adaptability of communities worldwide. This change can largely be attributed to environmental degradation from the exploitation of natural resources (e.g. Meyer and Turner, 1992; Dobson et al., 1997; Coleman and Williams, 2002) and the alteration of the earth's climate system through unnatural amounts of greenhouse gas (GHG) emissions into the atmosphere (e.g. IPCC, 2001; 2007). Focus on global climate change and its attributed environmental and socio-economic consequences over past decades, particularly over the last several years, has led to a growing body of literature and increasing concern about climate change impacts on human populations (e.g. Adger et al., 2003; IPCC, 2007; van Aalst et al., 2008).

Highly uncertain risks are expected to affect many dimensions of societies (i.e. agriculture, fisheries, energy, tourism, forestry, water resources, etc.) that are essential to the livelihoods of human populations, particularly in developing countries. For societies already vulnerable and sensitive to external stresses, climate change risks may exacerbate the social and economic conditions

■ *Corresponding author. *E-mail:* william.collier@yale.edu

ENVIRONMENTAL HAZARDS 8 (2009) 171–186
doi:10.3763/ehaz.2009.0021 © 2009 Earthscan ISSN: 1747-7891 (print), 1878-0059 (online) www.earthscanjournals.com earthscan

they face (Adger et al., 2003; Suárez et al., 2005). However, both contemporary and historical case studies, especially those in Africa and Asia-Pacific, have demonstrated that resilience is strong. Yet populations and communities have a new challenge to face that will certainly test this resilience.

The rate of change driven by increased anthropogenic GHG emissions continues to accelerate faster than previously anticipated (IPCC 2007; Rahmstorf et al., 2007; Smith et al., 2009). This is illustrated by one of the manifestations of climate change, the increasing intensity and frequency of natural disasters and extreme weather events (Srinivas and Nakagawa, 2008; Smith et al., 2009). The rate of increase of disasters as well as the numbers of people affected by these hazard events has been dramatic over the past decade (IFRC, 2003). Thus, the urgency to respond to these changes, even in the face of uncertainty, has become much more pressing and presents the need for assisted adaptation.

These recent trends have placed disasters at the centre of human–environment debates and have linked them with issues of development, technology and economic resiliency (Schipper and Pelling, 2006). As a response to this concern, international governance bodies, national governments, development agencies and organizations, non-governmental and non-profit organizations and private enterprise are creating mitigative and adaptive responses to these issues (Smit and Wandel, 2006). Special attention has been given to developing nations, which are considered to be the most vulnerable to the risks and pressures exerted by environmental change. In order to confront this, research endeavours, policies and practices that enhance resilience must be considered as a way to respond to a world that is in constant change (Pelling and Uitto, 2001).

In this article, we review the current understanding of natural and social disasters, the paradigm shifts in disaster management, the emergence of climate change adaptation (CCA) and the linkages between CCA and disaster risk reduction (DRR). Current scholarly and practitioner attempts to link the two fields are described, and we propose an urgent need for a holistic and dynamic systems approach, focusing on socio-ecological resilience as an opportunity to increase collaboration between the fields. We suggest two mechanisms to achieve this: (1) the use of iterative risk management as a primary instrument for adaptive decision making and (2) the establishment of boundary organizations and institutional changes to increase the transfer of knowledge between science, policy and practice.

The thoughts presented throughout this review are informed by a recent Forum held on 23–24 April 2009 at the Yale School of Forestry and Environmental Studies, entitled 'A Dynamic Systems Approach to Socio-ecological Resilience and Disaster Risk Reduction: Prioritizing the Gaps in a Changing World'. The two-day event covered many aspects of CCA, DRR and socio-ecological resilience. The participants, who are researchers, practitioners and policy makers, were charged with crossing traditional disciplines and boundaries to indentify and prioritize gaps and ways forward to link the fields of CCA and DRR for a holistic systems approach to deal with the inherent uncertainty associated with climate change and hazard events.

1.1. Understanding natural and social disasters

There is a significant body of literature regarding conceptualizations and definitions of disasters in the social science literature (e.g. Quarantelli and Dynes, 1977; Turner and Pidgeon, 1978; Quarantelli, 1988; 1998; Oliver-Smith, 1996). One such example is Oliver-Smith (1996, p. 303) who defines disasters as 'a process or event involving a combination of a potentially destructive agent(s) from the natural and/or technological environment and a population in a socially and technologically produced state of vulnerability'. Thus, natural disasters are the result of the interaction between a vulnerable population and a hazard event. Consequently, climate change will have a twofold effect on disaster risk: (1) through the increase in weather and climate hazards, and (2) through an increase in social vulnerability to these hazards. By exacerbating ecosystem degradation and affecting livelihoods at the local level, climate change will become an additional stressor as well as an inhibitor for communities' coping capacity (ISDR, 2002).

High vulnerability and low adaptive capacity have been associated with societies with a high dependence on natural resources (World Bank, 2000). This echoes the concern of the Intergovernmental Panel on Climate Change (IPCC) for low-lying coastal and island regions whose populations are highly reliant on natural resources; current adaptation for these communities is unbalanced and 'readiness for increased exposure is low' (IPCC, 2007, p. 15). Many of these regions are the most disaster-prone in the world and have experienced disaster relief and development interventions for decades. Yet resilience is still considered low in these countries. The lingering question, therefore, is 'why?' We will return to this question in detail later, but will first supply a background of the emergence of several important paradigm shifts.

1.2. From disaster response to disaster risk reduction

Since the 1970s, the disaster relief and humanitarian community has gone through several important paradigm shifts. The community, over the years, has refined its understanding and management of disasters, from identifying and responding to hazard events to determining and targeting the underlying drivers of vulnerability that turn hazards into disasters. Although the shifts are more recent, Carr (1932) proposed the conceptual model for many of these ideas much earlier. An important shift in the practitioner community came in the early 1980s, when the US Federal Emergency Management Agency (FEMA) proposed an approach to disaster management that distinguished between mitigation, preparedness, response and recovery. Similarly, following the International Decade for Natural Disaster Reduction (IDNDR) (1990–1999), the United Nations International Strategy for Disaster Reduction (ISDR) was mandated to focus on

the paradigm shift from disaster mitigation to disaster prevention, also known as DRR. At the interim of the IDNDR, the Yokohama Strategy and Plan of Action for a Safer World led to a change in thinking about disaster mitigation (Schipper and Pelling, 2006). Movement in thinking and practice continued during the United Nations World Conference on Disaster Reduction (WCDR) in 2005 (Schipper and Pelling, 2006). As a result, the Hyogo Framework for Action (HFA) (2005–2015) was established as an international commitment providing technical and political agreement on issues necessary to reduce disaster risk. Ultimately, these shifts led to the newly recognized DRR framework. ISDR promoted this framework to development and humanitarian organizations worldwide. The combined efforts of various stakeholders produced an increasing desire to identify actions that promote reducing vulnerability before hazards can result in undesirable impacts, particularly within the context of climate change (Klein et al., 2003). This interest continues to date. In fact, the forthcoming IPCC Assessment Report (AR5) will have a distinct chapter on DRR as an adaptation strategy, and the IPCC is also developing a Special Report on managing the risks of extreme events and hazards, focusing largely on DRR (IISD, 2009).

Despite the efforts of the past several decades, including preventative measures that have been demonstrated to be more economically efficient than reactive ones, disaster relief, response and recovery still predominate. This is also discouraging because a growing body of literature suggests that post-disaster response can actually increase vulnerabilities in the long term (Anderson and Woodrow, 1998; Schipper and Pelling, 2006).

Nonetheless, as the emphasis continues to shift from disaster response to DRR, greater and sustained efforts are needed to make these changes within research institutions as well as development and humanitarian agencies and organizations (Linnerooth-Bayer et al., 2005). In such efforts, many institutions, agencies and organizations are developing analytical tools for disaster management, to identify indicators for effective disaster preparedness in the hopes of helping communities to reduce their risk from disasters. Likewise, Schipper and Pelling (2006) suggest that such risk appraisal and assessment methodologies could prove significant in designing development strategies in the future.

1.3. The emergence of climate change adaptation

CCA emerged from the international treaty of the UN Framework Convention on Climate Change (UNFCCC) in 1992, especially for developing country parties through Article 4. CCA has been given second priority to climate change mitigation (CCM) since its inception, however, because of a perceived sense of greater urgency to slow the pace of emissions in response to Article 2 obligations about avoiding dangerous anthropogenic interference to the climate system (Pielke, 1998; Schipper and Pelling, 2006). For example, the Kyoto Protocol (2008–2012), an international agreement linked to the UNFCCC, sets legally binding targets for the reduction of GHG emissions but has only little emphasis on CCA. Many parties have disagreed on this prioritization, notably developing countries.

Limited success to date in CCM and increased clarity in climate change signals have made parties realize the importance and parallel urgency of adaptive measures and policies. Indeed, IPCC (2007) concludes that observed impacts from climate change to which the planet is already committed would continue throughout the next century even if GHG emissions were cut to zero. So, while CCM has traditionally been the pivotal issue for many climate change experts, CCA is now widely acknowledged as necessary for responding effectively and equitably to the impacts of climate change. In recent years, CCA has become a key focus of the scientific and policy-making communities and is now a major area of discussion under the UNFCCC. The Seventh Conference of the Parties (COP7) in 2001 addressed the special concerns of the world's 38 Least Developed Countries (LDCs), which were given an opportunity to develop National Adaptation Programmes of Action (NAPAs). Similarly, at the Eleventh Conference of the Parties (COP11) in 2005 the Nairobi Work Programme (NWP) (2005–2010) was established to focus exclusively on impacts, vulnerabilities and adaptation. CCA gained further recognition at the Thirteenth Conference of the Parties (COP13) in 2007 when the Bali Road Map (BRM) and Bali Action Plan (BAP), which chart a path to move forward post-Kyoto Protocol, gave equal priority to both CCM and CCA. The BAP also identified risk management and DRR as important elements for CCA moving forward.

Governments, institutions, researchers, practitioners and populations are all preparing for the CCA challenge posed to societies. In such efforts, Klein and Tol (1997) and Huq and Klein (2003) have developed approaches to anticipatory adaptation. Increased importance of CCA and identification of DRR has led to numerous initiatives that address both DRR and CCA (e.g. UNISDR Working Group on Climate Change and the Red Cross/Red Crescent Climate Change Center), suggesting that DRR has much to contribute to CCA policy and research (Handmer, 2003).

Community-based adaptation (CBA) is one innovative approach to CCA that focuses on enabling communities to enhance their own adaptive capacity, thereby empowering vulnerable communities to increase their own resilience to the impacts of climate change. CBA identifies, assists and implements community-based activities, research and policy in regions where adaptive capacity is as dependent on livelihoods as climatic changes. While CBA has strong merits for strengthening the resilience of communities, it cannot, however, be viewed as a panacea. We propose, as have others (e.g. O'Brien et al., 2006; Schipper and Pelling 2006; Thomalla et al., 2006), that CCA and DRR must to be integrated together into a larger, holistic and systems-based approach, and that CBA techniques could play an important role in achieving many of the desired goals towards increasing socio-ecological resilience and reducing disaster risk.

2. Linking disaster risk reduction and climate change adaptation

It has become apparent that climate change will not only be expressed through slow-onset changes in trends and average conditions over a long period, but also through non-linear and stochastic shifts in the frequency, intensity and severity of extreme events. The disaster relief community has great experience with droughts, floods, heat waves and cyclones, but only recently have disaster scholars and practitioners engaged in climate change debates (Helmer and Hilhorst, 2006). One of the most evident distinctions between DRR and CCA is that, while CCA focuses solely on the disturbances attributed to the dynamic climate system, DRR deals with all types of hazards, which include geophysical hazards as well (Schipper and Pelling, 2006). Both stress recent emphasis of working with communities, either by addressing risk aspects of climate change (in the case of DRR) or increasing resilience through CBA (in the case of CCA) (Næss et al., 2005; Tompkins, 2005; Penning-Rowsell, 2006). In attempts to link the two fields, it is noted that the 'core insight disaster studies can bring to climate-related research is that vulnerability is critical to discerning the nature of disasters' (Helmer and Hilhorst, 2006, p. 2). Thus, as the intensity and frequency of disasters increases, it becomes a requirement for DRR and CCA also to increase resilience (Helmer and Hilhorst, 2006, p. 3).

The IPCC Fourth Assessment Report (AR4) (2007) identifies the usefulness of taking a risk perspective in order to identify synergies to 'promote sustainable development, reduce the risk of climate-related damage, and take advantage of climate-related opportunities'. For years, the UNISDR was internally attempting to link CCA and DRR and until recently was largely unsuccessful. On 29 September 2008, the UN Secretary General Ban Ki-Moon made the following statement at a ministerial meeting he specially convened in New York:

If we are too slow to adapt to climate change, we risk making disasters even more catastrophic than they need to be. We must draw on the Hyogo Framework for Action and disaster risk reduction knowledge to protect the world's most vulnerable populations against climate change (Ban Ki-Moon, 2008).

This meeting officially linked the UN programme areas of CCA and DRR at the international level. Furthermore, at this meeting the Secretary General called on ministers to lead the way at the UNFCCC negotiations by championing DRR as a core element of CCA. This was a critical step for developing countries and has opened the door for collaboration between the two disciplines to share much-needed resources, ultimately leading towards more effective protection of the most vulnerable populations. While DRR is relatively new and constantly developing new methods, CCA is even younger. At this early stage of development, the integration of these two fields holds significant potential to address the impacts of climate change and reduce vulnerable populations' risk from disaster.

Most importantly though, while there have been some notable exceptions, few research initiatives are actually aimed at answering practitioner questions (Helmer and Hilhorst, 2006). We defer to Kellenberg and Mobarak (2008) to illustrate an exception that addresses an important practitioner concern. The authors show that previous literature and understanding on the negative relationship between income per capita and measures of risk from natural disasters missed an important point: behavioural changes at the microlevel in response to increasing income may lead to a nonlinear relationship between aggregating incomes and disaster damages, where risks increase with income before they decrease. This suggests that the dual goals of DRR and economic development cannot be assumed to be complementary for all forms of natural disasters, specifically flooding, landslides and windstorms. Extreme temperature events and earthquakes seem to follow the traditional thought more closely. This has significant policy and practical implications for developing, and particularly least developed, countries. To again elucidate the link to CCA, those divergent disasters (i.e. flooding, landslides and windstorms) are all hazards that projections show will increase with climate change (IPCC, 2007).

3. Resilience as a dynamic systems concept

A detailed body of literature over previous decades has shown that many of the world's ecological problems originate from social problems, especially under dominant and hierarchal sociopolitical regimes. Consequently, in order to understand and deal with ecological problems, societal problems must be addressed. In considering socio-ecological systems, socio-economic resilience may be considered to have a higher impact than biophysical resilience (Young et al., 2006).

Traditionally, research on adaptation to environmental change has been centred on the *responses* of different social entities to environmental stimuli. Alternatively, the resilience approach is based on a holistic perspective that *anticipates* dynamic change and views adaptive capacity as an essential characteristic of socioecological systems. The resilience approach also provides a framework through which CCA processes can be analysed and policies can be identified. The approach allows for greater flexibility in CCA, since it envisions the possibility of change in the state of systems itself. Thus, the approach fosters the prevalence of those characteristics that allow the system to assimilate perturbations without losing their autonomy (i.e. function, networks, social capital, etc.) in a dynamic environment (Nelson et al., 2007). Folke states:

> The implication for policy is profound and requires a shift in mental models toward human-in-the-environment perspectives, acceptance of the limitation of policies based on steady-state thinking and design of incentives that stimulate the emergence of adaptive governance for social-ecological resilience of landscapes and seascapes (Folke, 2006, p. 263).

The term resilience has been used metaphorically in a socio-ecological context since the 1970s. Almost four decades later, there seems to have been little clarity attained in regard to what makes a system resilient or how resilience can be enhanced (Klein et al., 2003). Some theorists use this term to refer to the ability of certain societies to adapt and cope with external shocks. In fact, in development practice it is widely assumed that a more resilient system is less vulnerable to hazards (Klein et al., 2003).

Holling (1973) first introduced the concept of a resilient ecosystem by defining it as a measure of the ability of ecosystems to absorb change and persist beyond that change. This work is highly valuable in that it contrasts the concept of resilience with that of stability. A stable ecosystem is one considered to return to a state of equilibrium after a temporary disturbance (Holling, 1973). Accordingly, a stable ecosystem would return to equilibrium quickly without major fluctuations, whereas a resilient system may reach high points of instability and fluctuation in a path towards dynamic change. This conceptualization is essential for applicability purposes, given the fact that systems, as we define them today, are dynamic and in constant change as they respond to both external and internal influences (Klein et al., 2003).

Carpenter et al. (2001) define resilience as the magnitude of disturbance that can be tolerated before a socio-ecological system moves into a different region of state-space controlled by a different set of processes. Accordingly, resilience may be considered in multiple contexts: in relation to sustainability, as a property of dynamic models and as a quantifiable variable that can be assessed through location-specific field studies. In order to accomplish this last point, there must be a general understanding of the socio-ecological system and disturbances must be identified (Carpenter et al., 2001).

As these ideas developed from an ecosystem perspective, resilience became a concept of value for economic and social studies as well. Certain ecological economists who considered resilience to be key to sustainability addressed the issues of a resilient society to climate change, hence linking resilience to vulnerability (Common, 1995; Klein et al., 2003).

The resilience concept was convergently developed in the context of disaster management. In this context, resilience is defined as the ability of a system (or one of its parts) to absorb and recover from the occurrence of a hazard event. Given the interest in the field of DRR to identify the qualities that minimize fatalities, Dovers and Handmer (1992) work within the conceptualization that resilience is critical. The authors distinguish between reactive and proactive resilience. In the former, a society aims to strengthen its status quo by promoting and enforcing the system's present characteristics. In the latter, change is integrated as an inevitable and intrinsic characteristic of systems, henceforth aiming efforts at creating a system that will be able to withstand change by adapting to the new conditions (Klein et al., 2003). As a result of these studies, Dovers and Handmer (1992) similarly identify the importance of resilience to the field of DRR in planning for and coping with disasters.

4. Linking resilience, vulnerability and adaptation

We have previously discussed synergies between CCA and DRR. Here, we attempt to further link the two fields through the complementary concepts of resilience and vulnerability. Resilience, vulnerability and adaptive capacity are mutually linked. As described by Smit and Wandel (2006), vulnerability of the system to a particular hazard is reflective of the system's exposure, sensitivity to the hazard and its resilience to the hazard. Adaptive capacity, or the ability of a system to adapt, defines the nature and state of adaptation towards a particular hazard. Thus, adaptive capacity of a system is closely dependent upon the resilience of the system.

Significant discussions on these concepts exist in the literature. While Turner et al. (2003) attribute coping capacity and adaptive capacity as separate dimensions of resilience, Smit and Wandel (2006) lump them together. To Smit and Wandel (2006), adaptive capacity is equivalent to resilience. Similarly, Dovers and Handmer (1992) suggest that proactive resilience is what should be termed as adaptive capacity, and Gallopín (2006) concludes that resilience is related to the capacity to respond. Despite important differences, in all these examples resilience is non-trivially related to adaptive capacity. Since, ultimately, CCA is a resultant of adaptive capacity, then the resilience of a system will certainly influence the CCA outcome.

In the context of DRR, conceptualizations of risks and disasters, including the pressure and release (PAR) model (Blaikie et al., 1994; Wisner et al., 2004), identify the environmental stresses of hazards and the progression of social forces that contribute to vulnerability, including those that relate to adaptive capacity. This view of socio-ecological coupled systems that specify the role of human adaptive responses is further developed in the vulnerability framework of Turner et al. (2003) and the access model of Wisner et al. (2004).

When addressing resilience, however, there are important questions to be addressed. For example, what is kept and what is lost when adapting? What is it, specifically, that should be resilient? Other questions in the literature emerge in respect to governance in socio-ecological systems. In particular, for whom is resilience to be managed, and for what purpose? (Lebel et al., 2006, p. 1). We refer to Lebel et al. (2006, p. 33), as they suggest that 'In our roles as analysts, facilitators, change agents, or stakeholders, we must ask not only: the resilience of what, to what? We must also ask: for whom?'

5. Uncertainty and iterative risk management

One of the greatest obstructions in understanding and combating climate change is the multitude of uncertainty surrounding climate change issues. From indentifying underlying drivers of vulnerability, to understanding the biophysical dynamics of the complex climate systems, to predicting and anticipating a variety of climate futures, one thing that is certain is that nothing will be certain when research agendas must be set, practical action must be applied and policy decisions must be made.

It is also important to recognize that systems consist of nested dynamics operating at multiple organizational scales. Thus, sub-systems exist within a given system and can have significant influence on overall resilience or vulnerability. This idea stresses the notion that socio-ecological systems are highly interconnected, forming networks of interaction at multiple scales.

In an attempt to understand such networks, Armitage et al. (2007) link the concepts of co-management and adaptive management to present a framework for both research and practice with a new term called 'adaptive co-management'. The authors state:

> The co-management narrative has been primarily concerned with user participation in decision making and with linking communities and government managers ... [while] the adaptive management narrative has been primarily about learning-by-doing in a scientific way to deal with uncertainty (Armitage et al., 2007).

Dynamic approaches to adaptive systems and complexity have catalysed insights in resource management and socio-ecological systems (Capra, 1996; Levin, 1999). Although adaptive co-management was primarily designed for natural resource management, we see it of equal importance to CCA and DRR, complementary at its roots to ideas of iterative risk management. Armitage et al. (2007) further assert of the breakdown of past assumptions in natural resource management that they:

> Are yielding to new developments and trends, including: (1) the imperative of broad-based participation when devising management strategies that respond to change; (2) the need to emphasize knowledge, learning and the social sources of adaptability, renewal and transformation; and (3) and understanding

of change and uncertainty as inherent in social-ecological systems.

This statement strongly reflects the convergent aspects of CCA and DRR. We see significant intersections in these fields, providing substantial opportunity to develop holistic, dynamic systems approaches to socio-ecological resilience.

The above supports the need for resilience approaches for institutional diversity. Iterative risk management is neither exclusively top-down nor bottom-up, but requires participatory approaches at all levels to gain a better understanding of a system. Specifically, iterative risk management should include both assessed risk *and* subjective risk. Furthermore, risk perception from local communities is essential for developing appropriate resilience-building strategies and participatory approaches that ensure local inclusion.

However, Ostrom et al. (2007) stress the importance of avoiding panaceas in community-based management, or any institution for that matter, to address issues of resilience. Allen (2006) similarly urges that community-based disaster preparedness (CBDP), which can be included in iterative risk management, cannot be treated as a panacea for disaster management. Both Ostrom et al. (2007) and Allen (2006), however, provide insightful works that highlight the merits and challenges of governance and community-based approaches to natural resource management and disaster preparedness. We suggest that these lessons can also be applied to iterative risk management and the resilience approaches to CCA and DRR.

Focusing on institutions while developing resilience strategies through iterative risk management raises an important complication. In particular, while institutional diversity and effectiveness can strengthen resilience, practitioners should be wary of and scientists should look for institutional forms that, although they may increase institutional performance, actually hinder resilience (Janssen and Anderies, 2007).

We propose that iterative risk management, and risk in general, is the appropriate lens through which to view uncertainty. IPCC (2007), similarly, concludes that iterative risk management is an appropriate approach to address climate change. However, there is still little information about what this means practically. Here, we attempt to elucidate what this means, and more importantly, how it might be implemented.

5.1. Risk and economic resilience

In a world where climate variability, extreme hazard events, robust ecosystem services and global financial markets are more and more uncertain, protecting financial assets in countries and communities becomes an imperative to ensure resilient societies. Economic and/or financial vulnerability can be reduced through a variety of mechanisms in terms of preparing for climate change. Some examples include promoting alternative livelihood awareness, developing income-generating adaptation efforts, conducting countrywide risk assessments that include financial vulnerability models, strengthening poverty reduction strategies, encouraging dual economies for local resource users and utilizing insurance schemes. By no means is this list exhaustive or are these concepts mutually exclusive. Below, we highlight how two of these approaches can strengthen economic resilience through iterative risk management.

ISDR (2009) recently released a report entitled *Risk and Poverty in a Changing Climate* that identifies three primary drivers of risk: (1) deficient urban and local governance, (2) vulnerable rural livelihoods, and (3) declining ecosystem services. Thus, to return to our earlier stated question, 'Why, with all the efforts of disaster relief, development intervention and local resource management, are communities still so vulnerable?' The ISDR (2009) report stressed that while disaster preparedness and response are reducing mortality, progress in tackling these three drivers of risk is insufficient.

We suggest that one approach to addressing these drivers is to link CCA and DRR with insurance mechanisms and other financial tools.

There is a significant body of literature exploring insurance for CCA and DRR (e.g. Kunreuther, 1996; Kunreuther and Michel-Kerjan, 2007) and insurance under uncertainty (e.g. Kunreuther, 1976; Schoemaker and Kunreuther, 1979; Hogarth and Kunreuther, 1985). However, there are also many challenges to effectively implementing insurance mechanisms for CCA and DRR, which Warner et al. (2009) identify as low awareness levels, lack of reliable information on risk pricing, accessibility, affordability and the potential for insurance to incentivize maladaptation. In many cases, direct investment (e.g. restoring mangroves) may be cheaper than insurance payouts. To overcome many of these challenges, we propose that countries, regions and insurers could make risk reduction activities a prerequisite to accessing insurance.

Insurance is largely based on the 'risk transfer principle', a fundamental tool for risk insurance schemes, especially for CCA in developing countries. Insurance companies spread consequences of a hazard event more evenly across an insured community. This explains why having large insured pools can make insurance more affordable and more effective. However, if losses resulting from climatic events become too frequent, intense, or severe, and all members of a community suffer damage, then there are no non-victims to share the burden. Insurance then becomes insolvent. For this reason, one goal of insurance companies is to ensure that damage does not become the norm. Therefore, CCA and DRR merged with insurance schemes could play an important role when discussing financial vulnerability and managing risks for governments and communities.

Understanding resilience and vulnerability is more complex than looking at risk, and there are strengths and weaknesses to this approach. As such, another challenge inherent to insurance is that of the 'moral hazard'. This occurs when the insured partake in risky behaviours instead of less risky behaviours because they feel protected by insurance. When intervening in communities that are hazard-prone, experience from insurance schemes shows that mechanisms should be put in place to avoid moral hazards. In the case of CCA and DRR insurance, one such mechanism, as suggested previously, is to make risk reduction a prerequisite for access to insurance. For resilience and vulnerability approaches, other mechanisms might include community empowerment, capacity building and awareness building.

After perturbations to a system, some communities have been forced to change their livelihood strategies, which are usually connected to an increase in risk. This was evident after the 1994 eruption of Mt Merapi in Central Java, Indonesia. A number of factors, including demographics, politics and the global economy, contributed to the village of Turgo shifting from a system wherein livestock supported subsistence agriculture to a system where agriculture supported market-oriented livestock husbandry (Dove and Hudayana, 2008). While this usually would increase risk because households become more dependent on external factors, in the case of the village of Turgo, risk was mitigated because market participation was limited to the sale of commodities and not the purchase of the inputs used in their production. As Dove and Hudayana (2008, p. 742) note, 'To continue reliance on local resources for agricultural production (viz. land, labor, livestock, vegetation) represents a significant buffer against market uncertainty and volatility'. By keeping one foot in traditional local subsistence living and one in global markets, the community created a dual economy that was able to mitigate risks associated with changing livelihoods after the eruption of Mt Merapi and subsequent government interventions. Thus, this duel economy increased the resilience of the socio-ecological system.

Yet, on a larger scale, there is the lack of a link to policy-relevant work with the inherent complexity of resilience and vulnerability. While there are relatively straightforward processes of doing risk planning, this is not the case for resilience planning. Therefore, we propose a nested approach at multiple scales, integrating iterative risk management within a resilience framework.

6. Information transfer and knowledge networks

A need has arisen to effectively utilize policies, programmes and institutional structures which are presently available, or which could be transferred from one sector to another, to strengthen the ability of societies to link CCA and DRR. This strongly relies on effective communication of information to be transferred and knowledge networks to be formed, both formally and informally. This can be accomplished through processes of social learning. According to Pelling et al. (2008), social learning has been interpreted within the literature to mean both individual learning that is conditioned by its social environment, and learning in the sense that social collectives such as organizations and institutions can 'learn' in their own right. These are distinct but complementary aspects of learning within organizations. The authors discern that since collaborative learning among peers facilitates learning, there is a possibility that informal 'communities of practice' can allow for knowledge to be diffused more efficiently and be more open (or in some cases, more constrained), thus impacting on the collective adaptive capacity of institutions, organizations and communities (Pelling et al., 2008).

An important component of social learning is facilitating useful knowledge networks and, moreover, identifying existing networks in order to support them through capacity building. Experience has shown that by making existing local networks more robust, a community, instead of outside 'experts', can sustain a project or programme more easily than a new network created by outside knowledge and expertise. Many communities have both formal institutions and networks such as government bodies, community organizations and customary laws, as well as informal networks that prove to be very effective during a disaster.

Special attention should also be given to the 'shadow systems' within organizations and communities, which allow individuals to affect organizational dynamics in an informal manner. Shadow systems, also referred to as 'informal institutions', are informal systems that are not regulated, do not represent formal roles, but often are dominant drivers of systems. These informal networks may imply that an organization could almost dissolve and still retain the original function of the organization. By enhancing the understanding of how these shadow systems and other institutional factors promote resilience, institutions and organizations could be reorganized and/or adjusted to accomplish our goals of strengthening systems resilience. Stacey (1996) and Shaw (1997) argue shadow systems significantly contribute to learning and innovation in organizations. A challenge is for organizations to support, without managing, these informal systems (Stacey, 1996; Shaw, 1997). This can also apply to shadow systems outside institutions and organizations, such as the shadow systems in local communities.

Few researchers have investigated the relationships between learning, communication and adaptive capacity. Yet, those that have argue that:

> Relational attributes of organizations and policy regimes allow individuals or sub-groups within organizations to experiment, imitate, communicate, learn and reflect on their actions in ways that can surpass formal processes within policy and organizational settings … offering a potential method for measuring adaptive capacity that focuses on process rather than output, enabling proactive adaptation (Pelling et al., 2008).

Studies further identify components of these concepts as (1) learning by doing, (2) integrating knowledge systems, (3) increasing collaboration and equity among community, regional and national levels, and (4) creating greater flexibility in management techniques (Olsson et al., 2004; Armitage et al., 2007). Again we see these proposals as complementary to the influence of social learning, knowledge networks and iterative risk management in linking CCA and DRR. Furthermore, we propose institutional changes, namely the creation of 'boundary organizations' as an important component of such efforts. Likewise, we suggest the development of innovative and layered institutions that facilitate learning

through change and complexity (as do Dietz et al., 2003).

We now return to the earlier question of 'why are communities still so vulnerable?' We propose another possible response, linked to our previous discussion. The use of iterative risk management, the efficient transfer of knowledge and development of knowledge networks described in the preceding sections, as well as the development of boundary organizations and institutional changes described in the following sections, all foster growth in underlying determinants of adaptive capacity. These range from governance issues, to recognizing and using human social capital, to understanding causal links and spreading risk to promote resilience, just to name a few. If the weakest link hypothesis proposed by Tol and Yohe (2007) holds true, then all these components are necessary to strengthen socio-ecological resilience. Up to now, disaster relief and development interventions have focused on one episode or one component at a time, ameliorating effects and events but not building support to lower vulnerability to future events. In short, weaknesses elsewhere have prevented increases in resilience because capacities have not increased.

7. Developing boundary organizations

The world has faced huge disasters over the last few decades and concerns have been expressed by nearly all international agencies involved that there is a scarcity of managerial skills to deal with the mitigation and management of disasters (Silva, 2001; APA, 2005; IRC, 2005; WHO, 2005; MacFarlane et al., 2006; UN Commissioner for Refugees, 2006). These skills are needed in both science and practice. We suggest that boundary organizations can fulfil this niche and are essential to achieve many objectives necessary to link CCA and DRR, such as utilizing iterative risk management and adaptive co-management, using a dynamic systems approach to socio-ecological resilience, and considering multiple scales when designing CCA and DRR strategies.

Yet, to date there is a lack of fluidity between research, policy and practice.

The term 'boundary organization' is not a new one. It has previously been used in the social sciences and environmental sciences, most often referred to as 'intermediate organizations' (Guston, 1995; 2001; Cash et al., 2002; 2006; Hellstrom and Jacob, 2003; Brooke, 2008). The Harvard University Global Environmental Assessment (GEA) Project defines such organizations as 'institutions that straddle the shifting divide between politics and science . . . It is hypothesized that the presence of boundary organizations facilitates the transfer of usable knowledge between science and policy' (Guston, 2001). Several examples of such institutions include the Sea Grant Program in the US, the Subsidiary Body for Scientific and Technological Advice (SBSTA) of the UNFCCC, the Stockholm Environment Institute, and ProVention Consortium of the World Bank.

Pointing out that science was traditionally kept separate to protect its legitimacy, Jasanoff's (1990) work on the advisory relationship between scientists and regulatory agencies demonstrated that blurring the boundaries between science and politics could lead to more productive policy making than could be achieved by maintaining intentional separation. While boundary organizations have not been extensively researched for CCA or DRR, there are some emerging exceptions. Brooke (2008) argues that 'boundary organizations – organizations or institutions that bridge different scales or mediate the relationship between science and policy – could prove useful for managing the transdisciplinary nature of adaptation to climate change, providing communication and brokerage services and helping to build adaptive capacity' in regards to biodiversity conservation and CCA. Another notable exception is Ludwig et al. (2009), who assert that 'climate-proofing requires, like other environmental problems, clearly (re)defined and negotiated boundaries between science and policy . . . problem-defining, policies and research agendas need to be mutually constructed in boundary organizations, which may also lie outside the traditional domain of water resources management' (Ludwig et al., 2009, p. 119). While related to CCA and DRR, these views of boundary organizations still seem to focus on science and policy, not science and practice. Thus, we argue, while human capital is improving, 'applicable' human capital lags behind.

The small difference between these previous definitions of boundary organizations and our current proposal is that Guston (2001) focuses on how science can guide policy making while not becoming politicized and Brooke (2008) focuses on biodiversity conservation and CCA and argues that non-governmental organizations are the appropriate actors to fill this niche because they tend to be active across the areas of science, policy and practice. Here, we propose the use of boundary organizations specifically to link CCA and DRR while arguing that a variety of existing institutions could be reorganized to fill this niche. We see boundary organizations as necessary to catalyse fluid communication and information transfer between science, policy *and* practice, not just science and policy. As Vogel et al. suggest:

> . . . Where the science–practice interaction is not taken seriously or carefully designed, a number of disconnections can emerge that frustrate otherwise well-meaning measures to reduce vulnerability and enhance resilience . . . thus, although there is a growing body of knowledge on vulnerability, adaptation, and resilience, and a variety of pressing application opportunities for that knowledge, all too often still silos of knowledge get produced that fail to help make systems and communities more robust to extremes and to change (Vogel et al., 2007, p. 352).

Additionally, it seems that most of the existing work on boundary organizations focuses on systematically incorporating scientific advice into the decision making of Western, democratized governing bodies and organizations. Furthermore, this body of work has focused heavily on formal institutions with multiple stakeholders in the Global North. Thus, emphasis has not been placed on the complex knowledge networks and informal institutions of communities in developing countries. We, therefore, see a need to extend these ideas to those institutions, communities and socio-ecological systems in the Global South.

8. Conclusions

Even though substantial discussion is taking place at the academic and policy levels in terms of incorporation and interaction of various concepts like CCA, DRR and socio-ecological resilience, very little has actually happened on the ground. We propose an urgent need for a dynamic systems approach to socio-ecological resilience as a primary objective for CCA and DRR. We furthermore suggest an immediate need for scholarly research to address the needs and concerns of practitioners on the ground. We have discussed two primary mechanisms to catalyse change in the fields of CCA and DRR. These include an increased use of iterative risk management for adaptive decision making and the establishment of boundary organizations and institutional changes that increase the transfer of knowledge between science, policy and practice.

As the boundaries between disciplines are linked, the traditional methods of quality control and scientific reward systems appear increasingly outdated. The conventional scientific institutional structures might require significant adjustment as researchers and practitioners attempt to cross disciplinary boundaries and the boundaries between science and practice. A dynamic systems approach to socio-ecological resilience may provide a significant opportunity to restructure institutions to fulfil this role. Embedding boundary organizations into academic institutions might be one way to deal with the institutional obstacle.

The Forum held on 23–24 April 2009 at the Yale School of Forestry and Environmental Studies, entitled 'A Dynamic Systems Approach to Socio-ecological Resilience and Disaster Risk Reduction: Prioritizing the Gaps in a Changing World', identified innovative and interdisciplinary scientific work as a key contributor to past and future resilience work. All participants in the Forum agreed that academic institutions and young scholars, respectively, provide significant opportunity to develop boundary organizations, as well as individuals who can work between disciplines and substantially increase communication between science, policy and practice.

Promoting a dynamic systems approach to socio-ecological resilience might provide the perfect opportunity to restructure the scientific institution, pave the way for a new generation of scholars, and increase collaboration between the young and the seasoned within academic institutions, development and relief organizations and government. We see this path, embedded in adaptive and iterative risk management, as the way forward for CCA and DRR.

Acknowledgements

Our deepest gratitude to all the participants of the Forum on socio-ecological resilience that informed this review article: W. Neil Adger, J. Marty Anderies, Margaret Arnold, Robert Bailis, Benjamin Cashore, Dhar Chakrabarti, Michael R. Dove, Janot-Reine Mendler de Suárez, Jacobo Ocharán, Chadwick Oliver, Elinor Ostrom, Mark Pelling, Reinhard Mechler, Pablo Suárez and Robert Watt. We also thank Boris Porfiriev for insightful comments during the review process. We would like to recognize the Yale School of Forestry and Environmental Studies, in particular James Gus Speth, Gordon Geballe and the dedicated graduate students, who all helped to make this endeavour a success. And finally, the Forum was made possible by the generous support of the Yale School of Forestry and Environmental Studies Student Affairs Committee, The Leitner Family Fund, the Yale Council on Latin American and Iberian Studies, the Yale Council on South Asian Studies, the Global Institute on Sustainable Forestry, Yale Forest Forum and the World Wildlife Fund. The views expressed in this article are solely those of the authors and do not reflect any views of the institutions and organizations mentioned above.

References

Adger, N. W., Huq, S., Brown, K., Conway, D. and Hulme, M., 2003. Adapting to climate change in the developing world. *Progress in Development Studies*, 3(3). 179–195.

Allen, K. M., 2006. Community-based disaster preparedness and climate adaptation: local capacity-building in the Philippines. *Disasters*, 30(1). 81–101.

Anderson, M. B. and Woodrow, P. J., 1998. *Rising from the Ashes*. Lynne Reiner Publishers, Boulder, CO.

APA (American Planning Association) New Orleans Planning Assessment Team, 2005. *Charting the Course for Rebuilding a Great American City – an Assessment of the Planning Function in Post-Katrina New Orleans*. American Planning Association. www.planning.org/katrina/pdf/rebuildingreport.pdf.

Armitage, D., Berkes, F. and Doubleday, N., 2007. *Adaptive Co-Management: Collaboration, Learning, and Multi-Level Governance*. University of British Columbia Press, Vancouver, BC.

Ban Ki-moon, 2008. www.unisdr.org/eng/media-room/media-room.htm.

Blaikie, P., Cannon, T., Davies, I. and Wisner, B., 1994. *At Risk: Natural Hazards, People's Vulnerability, and Disasters* (1st edn). Routledge, London.

Brooke, C., 2008. Conservation and adaptation to climate change. *Conservation Biology*, 22(6). 1471–1476.

Capra, F., 1996. *The Web of Life: A New Scientific Understanding of Living Systems*. Doubleday, New York, NY.

Carpenter, S., Walker, B., Anderies, J. M. and Abel, N., 2001. From metaphor to measurement: resilience of what to what? *Ecosystems*, 4(8). 765–781.

Carr, L. J., 1932. Disaster and the sequence-pattern concept of social change. *American Journal of Sociology*, 38(2). 207–218.

Cash, D. W., Clark, W. C., Alcock, F., Dickson, N., Eckley, N., Guston, D. H., Jäger, J. and Mitchell, R. B., 2002. Knowledge systems for sustainable development. *Proceedings of the National Academy of Sciences USA*, 100. 8086–8091.

Cash, D. W., Adger, W. N., Berkes, F., Garden, P., Lebel, L., Olsson, P., Pritchard, L. and Young, O., 2006. Scale and cross-scale dynamics: governance and information in a multilevel world. *Ecology and Society*, 11(2). 8.

Coleman, F. C. and Williams, S. L., 2002. Overexploiting marine ecosystem engineers: potential consequences for biodiversity. *Trends in Ecology and Evolution*, 17(1). 40–44.

Common, M., 1995. Economists don't read Science. *Ecological Economics*, 15(2). 101–103.

Dietz, T., Ostrom, E. and Stern, P., 2003. The struggle to govern the commons. *Science*, 302(5652). 1907–1912.

Dobson, A. P., Bradshaw, A. D. and Baker, A. J. M., 1997. Hopes for the future: restoration ecology and conservation biology. *Science*, 277(5325). 515–522.

Dove, M. R. and Hudayana, B., 2008. The view from the volcano: an appreciation of the work of Piers Blaikie. *Geoforum*, 39. 736–746.

Dovers, S. R. and Handmer, J. W., 1992. Uncertainty, sustainability, and change. *Global Environmental Change*, 2(4). 262–276.

Folke, C., 2006. Resilience: the emergence of a perspective for socio-ecological systems analyses. *Global Environmental Change*, 16(3). 253–267.

Gallopín, G. C., 2006. Linkages between vulnerability, resilience, and adaptive capacity. *Global Environmental Change*, 16(3). 293–303.

Guston, D. H., 1995. Five tensions between science and democracy. *Forum Proceedings: Vannevar Bush II Science for the 21st Century*. 239–242.

Guston, D. H., 2001. Boundary organizations in environmental policy and science: an introduction. *Science, Technology, and Human Values*, 26. 87–112.

Handmer, J. W., 2003. We are all vulnerable. *Australian Journal of Emergency Management*, 18. 55–59.

Hellstrom, T. and Jacob, M., 2003. Boundary organizations in science: from discourse to construction. *Science and Public Policy*, 30(4). 235.

Helmer, M. and Hilhorst, D. J. M., 2006. Natural disasters and climate change. *Disasters*, 30(1). 1–4.

Hogarth, R. M. and Kunreuther, H. C., 1985. Ambiguity and insurance decisions. *American Economic Review*, 75(2). 386–390.

Holling, C. S., 1973. Resilience and stability of ecological systems. *Annual Review of Ecology and Systematics*, 4. 1–23.

Huq, S. and Klein, R. J. T., 2003. *Adaptation to Climate Change: Why and How*. SciDev.Net Climate Change Dossier, Policy brief. www.scidev.net/dossiers/index.cfm?fuseaction=printarticle&dossier=4&policy=44.

IFRC (International Federation of the Red Cross and Red Crescent Societies), 2003. *World Disasters Report 2003*. Oxford University Press, Oxford.

IISD (International Institute for Sustainable Development), 2009. *IPCC to Prepare Special Report on Extreme Events and Disasters.* IISD Reporting Services. http://climate-l.org/2009/04/29/ipcc-to-prepare-special-report-on-extreme-events-and-disasters/.

IPCC (Intergovernmental Panel on Climate Change), 2001. *Climate Change 2001: Impacts, Adaptation and Vulnerability. Contribution of Working Group II to the Third Assessment Report of the Intergovernmental Panel on Climate Change.* Cambridge University Press, Cambridge, UK.

IPCC (Intergovernmental Panel on Climate Change), 2007. *Climate Change 2007: Impacts, Adaptation and Vulnerability. Contribution of Working Group II to the Third Assessment Report of the Intergovernmental Panel on Climate Change.* Cambridge University Press, Cambridge, UK.

IRC (International Rescue Committee), 2005. *Programme Update – Somalia.* International Federation of Red Cross and Red Crescent Societies. www.ifrc.org/docs/appeals/annual05/05AA00201.pdf.

ISDR (International Strategy for Disaster Reduction), 2002. *Living with Risk: A Global Review of Disaster Reduction Initiatives.* United Nations, Geneva, Switzerland.

ISDR, 2009. *Global Assessment Report on Disaster Risk Reduction: Risk and Poverty in a Changing Climate.* United Nations, Geneva, Switzerland.

Janssen, M. A. and Anderies, J. M., 2007. Robustness trade-offs in socio-ecological systems. *International Journal of the Commons*, 1(1). 77–99.

Jasanoff, S., 1990. *The Fifth Branch: Science Advisers as Policymakers.* Harvard University Press, Cambridge, MA.

Kellenberg, D. and Mobarak, A. M., 2008. Does rising income increase or decrease damage risk from natural disasters? *Journal of Urban Economics*, 63(3). 788–802.

Klein, R. J. T. and Tol, R. J. S., 1997. Adaptation to climate change: options and technologies – an overview paper. *Technical Paper FCCC/TP/1997/3.* UNFCCC (United Nations Framework Convention on Climate Change) Secretariat, Bonn, Germany.

Klein, R. J. T., Nicholls, R. J. and Thomall, F., 2003. Resilience to natural hazards: how useful is this concept? *Environmental Hazards*, 5. 35–45.

Kunreuther, H. C., 1976. Limited knowledge and insurance protection. *Public Policy*, 24(2). 227–261.

Kunreuther, H. C., 1996. Mitigating disaster losses through insurance. *Journal of Risk and Uncertainty*, 12. 171–187.

Kunreuther, H. C. and Michel-Kerjan, E. O., 2007. Climate change, insurability of large-scale disasters, and the emerging liability challenge. *University of Pennsylvania Law Review*, 155(6). 1795–1842.

Lebel, L., Anderies, J. M., Campbell, B., Folke, C., Hatfield-Dodds, S., Hughes, T. P. and Wilson, J., 2006. Governance and the capacity to manage resilience in regional social-ecological systems. *Ecology and Society*, 11(1). 19.

Levin, S. A., 1999. *Fragile Dominion: Complexity and the Commons.* Perseus Books, Reading, MA.

Linnerooth-Bayer, J., Mechler, R. and Pflug, G., 2005. Refocusing disaster aid. *Science*, 309. 1044–1046.

Ludwig, F., Kabat, P. and van Schaik, H., 2009. *Climate Change Adaptation in the Water Sector.* Earthscan, London.

MacFarlane, C., Joffe, A. L. and Naidoo, S., 2006. Training of disaster managers at a masters degree level: from emergency care to managerial control. *Emergency Medicine Australasia*, 18. 451–456.

Meyer, W. B. and Turner, B. L., 1992. Human-population growth and global land-use cover change. *Annual Review of Ecology and Systematics*, 23. 39–61.

Næss, L. O., Bang, G., Eriksen, S. and Vevatne, J., 2005. Institutional adaptation to climate change: flood responses at the municipal level in Norway. *Global Environmental Change*, 15(2). 125–138.

Nelson, D. R., Adger, W. N. and Brown, K., 2007. Adaptation to environmental change: contributions of a resilience framework. *Annual Review of Environment and Resources*, 32. 395–419.

O'Brien, G., O'Keefe, P., Rose, J. and Wisner, B., 2006. Climate change and disaster management. *Disasters*, 30(1). 64–80.

Oliver-Smith, A., 1996. Anthropological research on hazards and disasters. *Annual Review of Anthropology*, 25. 303–328.

Olsson, P., Folke, C. and Berkes, F., 2004. Adaptive co-management for building resilience in social-ecological systems. *Environmental Management*, 34(1). 75–90.

Ostrom, E., Janssen, M. A. and Anderies, J. M., 2007. Going beyond panaceas. *Proceedings of the National Academy of Sciences of the United States of America*, 104(39). 15176–15178.

Pelling, M. and Uitto, J. I., 2001. Small island developing states: natural disaster vulnerability and global change. *Environmental Hazards*, 3. 49–62.

Pelling, M., High, C., Dearing, J. and Smith, D., 2008. Shadow spaces for social learning: a relational understanding of adaptive capacity to climate change within organizations. *Environment and Planning*, 40(4). 867–884.

Penning-Rowsell, E., 2006. 'Signals' from pre-crisis discourse: lessons from UK flooding for global environmental policy change? *Global Environmental Change*, 16. 323–339.

Pielke, R. A., 1998. Rethinking the role of adaptation in climate policy. *Global Environmental Change*, 8(2). 159–170.

Quarantelli, E. L., 1988. Disaster crisis management – a summary of research findings. *Journal of Management Studies*, 25(4). 373–385.

Quarantelli, E. L., 1998. *What is a Disaster? Perspectives on the Question.* Routledge, New York, NY.

Quarantelli, E. L. and Dynes, R. R., 1977. Response to social crisis and disaster. *Annual Review of Sociology*, 3. 23–49.

Rahmstorf, S., Cazenave, A., Church, J. A., Hansen, J. E., Keeling, R. F., Parker, D. E. and Somerville, R. C. J., 2007. Brevia: recent climate observations compared to projections. *Science*, 316(5825). 709.

Schipper, L. and Pelling, M., 2006. Disaster risk, climate change, and international development: scope for, and challenges to, integration. *Disasters*, 30(1). 19–38.

Schoemaker, P. J. H. and Kunreuther, H. C., 1979. An experimental study of insurance decisions. *Journal of Risk and Insurance*, 46(4). 603–618.

Shaw, P., 1997. Intervening in the shadow systems of organizations – consulting from a complex perspective. *Journal of Organizational Chain Management*, 10(3). 235.

Silva, A., 2001. *Floods in Mozambique – Emergency Health Report.* WHO.

Smit, B. and Wandel, J., 2006. Adaptation, adaptive capacity and vulnerability. *Global Environmental Change*, 16(3). 282–292.

Smith, J. B., Schneider, S. H., Oppenheimer, M., Yohe, G. W., Hare, W., Mastrandrea, M. D., Patwardhan, A., Burton, I., Corfee-Morlot, J., Magadza, C. H. D., Füssel, H. -M., Pittock, A. B., Rahman, A., Suarez, A. and van Ypersele, J. -P., 2009. Assessing dangerous climate change through an update of the Intergovernmental Panel on Climate Change (IPCC) 'reasons for concern'. *Proceedings of the National Academy of Sciences*, 106(11). 4133–4137.

Srinivas, H. and Nakagawa, Y., 2008. Environmental implications for disaster preparedness: lessons learnt from the Indian Ocean Tsunami. *Journal of Environmental Management*, 89. 4–13.

Stacey, R. D., 1996. *Complexity and Creativity in Organizations.* Berett-Koehler Publishers, San Francisco, CA.

Suárez, P., Anderson, W., Mahal, V. and Lakshmanan, L., 2005. Impacts of flooding and climate change on urban transportation: a systemwide performance assessment of the Boston Metro Area. *Transportation Research*, 10. 231–244.

Thomalla, F., Downing, T., Spanger-Siegfried, E., Han, G. and Rockström, J., 2006. Reducing hazard vulnerability: towards a common approach between disaster risk reduction and climate change adaptation. *Disasters*, 30(1). 39–48.

Tol, R. S. J. and Yohe, G. W., 2007. The weakest link hypothesis for adaptive capacity: an empirical test. *Global Environmental Change*, 17(2). 218–227.

Tompkins, E. L., 2005. Planning for climate change in small islands: insights from national hurricane preparedness in the Cayman Islands. *Global Environmental Change*, 15(2). 139–149.

Turner, B. A. and Pidgeon, N., 1978. *Man-made Disasters: The Failure of Foresight.* Taylor and Francis, London.

Turner, II B. L., Kasperson, R. E., Matson, P. A., McCarthy, J. J., Corell, R. W., Christensen, L., Eckley, N., Kasperson, J. X., Luers, A., Martello, M. L., Polsky, C., Pulsipher, A. and Schiller, A., 2003. A framework for vulnerability analysis in sustainability science. *Proceedings of the National Academy of Sciences USA*, 100(14). 8074–8079.

UN Commissioner for Refugees, 2006. *The State of the World's Refugees 2006 – Human Displacement in the New Millennium.* Oxford University Press, Oxford, UK.

van Aalst, M. K., Cannon, T. and Burton, I., 2008. Community level adaptation to climate change: the potential role of participatory community risk assessment. *Global Environmental Change*, 18. 165–179.

Vogel, C., Moser, S. C., Kasperson, R. E. and Dabelko, G. D., 2007. Linking vulnerability, adaptation, and resilience science to practice: pathways, players and partnerships. *Global Environmental Change*, 17. 349–364.

Warner, K., Ranger, N., Surminski, S., Arnold, M., Linnerooth-Bayer, J., Michael-Kerjan, E., Kovacs, P. and Herweijer, C., 2009. *Adaptation to Climate Change: Linking Disaster Risk Reduction and Insurance.* United Nations ISDR (International Strategy for Disaster Reduction) Secretariat, Geneva, Switzerland.

WHO (World Health Organization) South East Asia, 2005. *Moving Beyond the Tsunami – The WHO Story.* World Health Organization, Geneva, Switzerland.

Wisner, B., Blaikie, P., Cannon, T. and Davies, I., 2004. *At Risk: Natural Hazards, People's Vulnerability and Disasters* (2nd edn). Routledge, London.

World Bank, 2000. *Can Africa Claim the 21st Century?* World Bank, Washington, DC.

Young, O. R., Berkhout, F., Gallopin, G. C., Janssen, M. A., Ostrom, E. and van der Leeuw, S., 2006. The globalization of socio-ecological systems: an agenda for scientific research. *Global Environmental Change*, 16. 304–316.

research article

ENVIRONMENTAL
HAZARDS
Human and Policy Dimensions

United States hurricane landfalls and damages: Can one- to five-year predictions beat climatology?

ROGER A. PIELKE JR*

Center for Science and Technology Policy Research, CIRES, University of Colorado-Boulder, 1333 Grandview Avenue, UCB 488, Boulder, CO 80309-0488, USA

This paper asks whether one- to five-year predictions of United States hurricane landfalls and damages improve upon a baseline expectation derived from the climatological record. The paper argues that the large diversity of available predictions means that some predictions will improve upon climatology, but for decades if not longer it will be impossible to know whether these improvements were due to chance or actual skill. A review of efforts to predict hurricane landfalls and damage on timescales of one to five years does not lend much optimism to such efforts in any case. For decision makers, the recommendation is to use climatology as a baseline expectation and to clearly identify hedges away from this baseline, in order to clearly distinguish empirical from non-empirical justifications for judgements of risk.

Keywords: economic damage; hurricanes; insurance; prediction; uncertainty

1. Introduction

The answer to the question posed in the subtitle is, unfortunately, no. This paper explains why skilful prediction of US hurricane landfalls and damages is not possible in the short term, defined here as a time period of one to five years. A 'skilful' prediction is one that improves upon expectations derived from the statistics of the long-term historical record.

More precisely, this paper argues that the range of predictive methodologies available, and the corresponding diversity of predictions, mean that it is guaranteed that some prediction(s) will beat climatology, but it will be many decades if ever before we can know if that performance was due to chance or actual skill in the prediction methodology. On the timescales of decision making, decision makers must therefore proceed under irreducible uncertainties and fundamental ignorance. There may be many reasons for decision makers to hedge their judgements of

risk in various directions, and there is ample science available to support virtually any hedging strategy. The paper concludes with a discussion of the implications of the lack of skilful prediction for decision making related to expectations of future storms and their impacts.

2. Methods and data

The methods employed in this paper are restricted to those that seek to identify strong signals using simple methods. This is for two reasons. First, strong signals identified using simple methods are most likely to have direct applications. There are countless studies that have sought to extract weak signals in messy hurricane data using complex methods, and such studies can indeed be of scientific value. However, for purposes of shaping expectations of hurricane behaviour on timescales of one to five years into the future, such studies are of little use if the signals identified

■ *E-mail: pielke@colorado.edu

ENVIRONMENTAL HAZARDS 8 (2009) 187–200

doi:10.3763/ehaz.2009.0017 © 2009 Earthscan ISSN: 1747-7891 (print), 1878-0059 (online) www.earthscanjournals.com

are dependent upon methodological choices or if the signal is small when compared to uncertainties or variability.

At times, when one reads studies seeking to identify patterns or causality in geophysical time series, one may be tempted to invoke the old saw about how tortured data will inevitably confess. But at the same time there may indeed be scientifically meaningful signals in the data that complex methods are able to extract. Regardless, it seems straightforward that the more difficult it is to identify a signal in messy data the less practically useful is that knowledge. In practical terms, on timescales of decision making a signal that cannot be seen is indistinguishable from a signal that does not exist. Second, there are a number of studies that have sought to use complex methods to identify patterns and relationships in the US hurricane landfall record. Those studies will be referenced here, but not replicated.

The data on the economic losses from US landfalling hurricanes comes from Pielke et al. (2008), which sought to adjust historical losses as recorded by the US National Hurricane Center to estimate the damage that each historical storm would have produced had it made landfall in 2005. Pielke et al. (2008) presented two methods for adjusting past losses. The data used in this paper are based on the method first introduced in Pielke and Landsea (1998), and have been updated through the 2008 hurricane season.[1] The data used here do not include damage from storms that made landfall at less than hurricane strength, though such damage is considered in Pielke et al. (2008).

The data on landfalling hurricanes is from the National Oceanic and Atmospheric Administration's Hurricane Reanalysis Project.[2] Various other data used in the analyses presented below will be cited as they are used. Information on landfalling hurricanes is generally recognized as being more reliable as long as a century ago and earlier because large tropical cyclones would have been difficult to miss as the coastline was becoming increasingly populated. However, in the Pielke et al. (2008) dataset there are six storms prior to 1940 which made landfall at hurricane strength

yet had no recorded damages. Logically, the chances that a landfalling storm was missed increases as one goes further back in time. However, the general convention is to assume that all landfalling hurricanes have been identified since 1900 (cf. Elsner and Jagger, 2006).

2.1. Landfall and damage records

Decision makers in a range of settings have considerable interest in the ability to anticipate hurricane landfalls in the USA and the losses associated with those impacts. Such expectations are key inputs to the pricing of homeowners' property insurance, the structure of complex financial transactions between global reinsurance firms and the movement of prices on commodities markets. Anticipation of hurricane landfalls can take the form of a prediction of a specific number of landfalls or the probability (risk) of landfalls. Judgements of risk are a form of prediction.

The US hurricane landfall record is shown in Figure 1 for the period 1851–2008 (reiterating that it is judged to be most accurate for the period since 1900, e.g. Landsea, 2007). The most important statistical feature of the record, since at least 1920, is its stationarity both in the number of storms making landfall (cf. Elsner and Bossack, 2001; Elsner et al., 2003; Nzerem et al., 2008; Smith, 2008) and also in the intensity of storms at landfall (Landsea, 2005). This means that the time series of landfalls has not shown any secular change although it has shown considerable variability. Thus, landfall statistics have been effectively modelled in various forms of a Poisson process (e.g. Elsner et al., 2003; Lu and Garrido, 2005). The damage record shows no trend since 1900 (Pielke et al., 2008). Average annual damage is USD11.3 billion (see Figure 2), and the median value is USD1.2 billion (updated to 2008 values); Pielke et al. (2008) provide a wide range of additional summary statistics and analysis of the normalized loss dataset.

The lack of trend in the landfall or damage record means that efforts to develop skilful

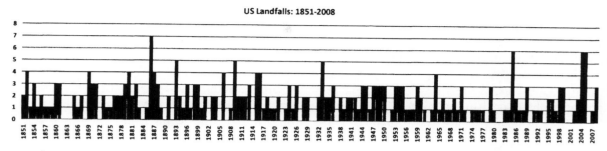

FIGURE 1 US hurricane landfalls, 1851–2008

predictions must necessarily be able to anticipate variability, as well as any future non-stationarities not evident in the historical record. If variability is to be anticipated then there must be relationships between those variables that can be accurately predicted and landfall frequency. Consequently, considerable scientific effort has been devoted to developing statistical and dynamic models of hurricane activity with the goal of offering skilful predictions of landfall

and thus impact. The following section reviews this literature.

3. Efforts to make connections

An ability to anticipate hurricane landfalls reliably on short timescales, such as five years or less, would be of considerable value to decision makers. Unfortunately, despite notable advances

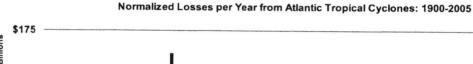
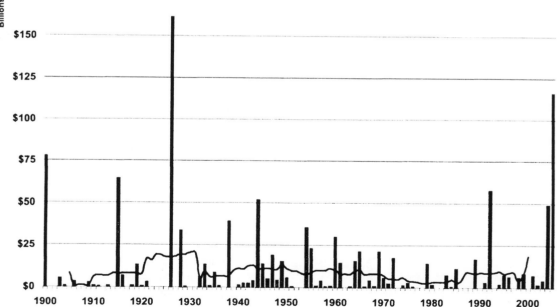

FIGURE 2 Normalized damages 1900–2005 for all landfalling tropical cyclones
Source: Reproduced from Pielke et al., 2008.

in scientific understanding as well as some indications of skilful in-sample explanatory power (i.e. retrodictions or hindcasts), no methodology has yet shown skilful out-of-sample predictions of US hurricane landfalls or damage, on timescales of one to five years, in the form of real-time forecasts provided to decision makers.

3.1. Landfall and North Atlantic Basin activity

Perhaps the most intuitive relationship to be explored is that between the total number of storms in the North Atlantic (NATL) and the number that make landfall. This relationship, however, is not straightforward. A simple correlation between the number of named storms (i.e. storms that reach tropical cyclone strength) and landfalling hurricanes is 0.46, explaining about 21 per cent of the variation in hurricane landfalls (for the period 1966–2008, which coincides with the satellite observational era; Landsea, 2007). Using only storms that reach hurricane strength in the correlation with landfalls offers a little improvement. Table 1 shows a range of simple correlations between basin activity, hurricane landfalls and damage.[3]

Logically, and as would be expected, correlations with damage improve as one moves to smaller subsets of the data, including intense hurricanes which historically have accounted for about 85 per cent of all damage (Pielke et al., 2008). The number of landfalling hurricanes shows a strong relationship with damage, explaining about half the variation and underscoring the importance of skilful landfall predictions. But at the same time, even a perfect prediction of the number of landfalling hurricanes leaves a considerable amount of uncertainty about damage, due to the nonlinear impacts of storms of different hurricane intensities, as well as the differential levels of population and development along the US coast.

Over decades it is clear that storm seasons with a greater number of named storms also have more landfalls and greater damage. From 1966 to 2008 hurricane seasons with 11 or more named storms (i.e. above the period average of 10.8 storms, which occurred in 23 of 43 years), there was an average of 2.1 US hurricane landfalls causing median damage of USD 2.3 billion. In seasons with 10 or fewer named storms (below the average of 10.8 storms, which occurred in 20 of 43 years) there was an average of 1.0 named storms causing median damage of USD640 million. However, the relationship between overall activity and landfalls is not nearly as pronounced in years with more than 11 named storms. The 13 years during the period 1966 to 2008 with 13 or more named storms had an average of 2.3 landfalling hurricanes, while the 10 years with 11 or 12 named storms had an average of 1.8 landfalling hurricanes. Each value falls well within the other's standard deviation, helping to explain why the overall number of named storms explains only a small portion of the variability in landfalls.

3.2. Landfall rates and proportion

Table 2 shows for three different periods – 1900–2008, 1951–2008 and 1979–2008 – the frequency of annual landfalls in the first and second half of each of the periods. A few curiosities stand out. The 54 years prior to 1954 saw 21 of 54 years (39 per cent) with zero or one landfall, whereas

TABLE 1 Correlations between various measures of activity, US landfalls and damage

	Hurricanes in basin	Landfalling hurricanes	Damage
Named storms in basin	0.87	0.46	0.27
Hurricanes in basin	*	0.52	0.42
Intense hurricanes in basin	*	0.58	0.45
Landfalling hurricanes	*	*	0.71

Note: Correlations with damage are computed as Spearman (rank) correlations. The time period of the analysis is 1966–2008, which coincides with the satellite observational era (Landsea, 2007).

TABLE 2 Number of years with indicated number of landfalls for three periods, each divided into halves

Hurricane landfalls	1900– 1953	1954– 2008	1951– 1979	1980– 2008	1979– 1993	1994– 2008
Zero	10	10	4	7	3	4
One	11	25	15	11	8	3
Two	17	7	3	4	1	3
Three	11	7	6	4	2	3
Four	3	0	0	0	0	0
Five	2	0	0	0	0	0
Six	0	3	0	3	1	2
Total years	54	54	29	29	15	15

the 54-year period 1954–2008 saw 35 years (65 per cent) with zero or one landfall. The 15-year period 1979–1993 saw four years with two or more landfalls, whereas the 15-year period 1994–2008 saw eight years with two or more landfalls. Damage from equal periods from 1901 to 2008 shows no evidence of secular changes in landfall numbers, overall damage or damage per landfall, as shown in Table 3 (cf. Pielke et al., 2008).

Efforts to anticipate future hurricane activity has primarily focused on developing seasonal predictions (i.e. for lead times of less than one year) of NATL basin activity, with yearly forecasts provided by teams from Colorado State University

TABLE 3 Landfalling hurricanes, total normalized damage and damage per landfall for four equal periods

	1901– 1927	1928– 1954	1955– 1981	1982– 2008
Landfalling hurricanes	48	54	37	48
Total normalized damage (USD billion)	296	296	205	349
Damage per landfall (USD billion)	6.2	5.5	5.5	7.3

Note: The data shown in Table 3 above are sensitive to choice of interval, given that large damaging events lead to a large fraction of the damage for any particular period. However, the choice of comparison period does not alter the perspective of a long-term stationarity in landfall and damage statistics. For instance, the 54-year period 1901–1954 saw USD592 billion in normalized damage from 101 landfalls and the 54-year period 1954–2008 saw USD554 billion in normalized damage from 83 landfalls.

and the National Oceanic and Atmospheric Administration, along with a range of scientists, private firms and consultants offering their own predictions (for a review, see Camargo et al., 2007). Even though such forecasts are announced with much fanfare, widely reported on in the media and considered by many decision makers, they have thus far offered very little insight to the subsequent season's landfall or damages.

Nonetheless, the changing number of storms in the NATL basin since 1995 as compared to a much quieter period from 1970 to 1994 has led to a vigorous scientific debate over hurricane landfalls. The data record for named storms in the NATL basin, unlike the landfall record, does indicate statistical non-stationarity over the 20th century and the latter half of the 19th century. Specifically it shows a long-term increase in the overall number of storms, punctuated by periods of greater and lesser activity (e.g. Holland and Webster, 2007; see also Briggs, 2008). The data record has led to several competing interpretations to explain why the basin statistics would show an increase while the landfall statistics would not.

The net result of the different behaviour of basin-wide activity and landfalling hurricanes is a decrease in the overall proportion of storms that make landfall, as shown in Figure 3, with a best fit linear trend. From at least 1950 there is no trend in the landfall proportion but considerable variation, ranging from 0 to about 55 per cent of named storms.

3.3. Spatial distribution of hurricane activity

One explanation for the different statistical behaviour of the basin and landfall data is that the increase observed in the overall basin activity is the result of changing observational practices rather than changes in storm activity. This line of argument posits, uncontroversially, that the number of landfalling storms is one of the most reliable hurricane time series. It then assumes, controversially, that the overall basin numbers are proportional to the number of landfalling

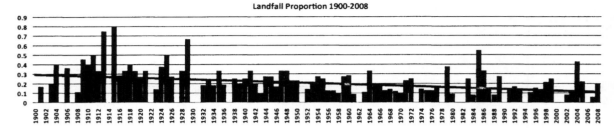

FIGURE 3 Proportion of named storms making landfall as hurricanes, 1900–2008

storms, and thus arrives at corrections which can be applied to the historical basin-wide data (examples of this line of argument can be found, for example, in Solow and Moore, 2002; Landsea, 2007).

A second line of argument is that the relatively small number of landfalls in the entire record leads to a meaningful chance that landfall numbers have indeed changed, based on the changes to overall basin activity, but that those changes cannot be detected at a statistically significant level. As Nzerem et al. (2008) argue, 'one cannot conclude from the lack of detectable change-points in the landfall series that this series isn't changing' (cf. Elsner et al., 2003). A similar line of argument was invoked by Emanuel (2005) in response to the observation that neither landfalls nor damage had increased since 1990 (Pielke, 2005). From the perspective of decision making, this argument is rather academic, as changes that cannot be detected can hardly be claimed to have much practical significance.

Both of these lines of argument miss an important factor in understanding the differential patterns seen in basin and landfall statistics, and that is the spatial distribution of trends in the NATL basin (see Pielke et al., 2008 for discussion). Specifically, if one looks at the increasing activity in the basin the increase has occurred in the easternmost part of the basin, far from land. The activity in areas where landfall takes place shows very similar trends to the landfall data. Figures 4a and 4b show these data.

Thus one need not invoke either the vagaries of chance or flawed data to explain the different statistics observed in the basin and for landfall. Instead, what needs to be explained is why the easternmost portion of the basin (i.e. the two most eastern quadrants in Figure 4b) has seen an increase in storm activity. This question will once again lead to thus-far unresolved questions about data quality and causality. However, because the activity in this part of the basin is not highly correlated with landfalls (Pielke and McIntyre, 2007), the debate is not particularly relevant to questions related to landfall prediction.

Because landfall proportions vary a great deal, even with a perfect prediction of basin activity, predictions of landfall will have limited skill. Thus, any prediction of landfall that assumes a constant landfall proportion (e.g. Coughlin et al., 2009) necessarily leads to a poor prediction of landfall activity. For instance, consider a prediction made starting in 2000 using data since 1950. If one compares a prediction of landfall based on simply the climatological average (from 1950 to the year before the predicted year) with a prediction using a perfect basin forecast assuming a constant landfall proportion (e.g. from 1950 to 1999, the average proportion was 15.6 per cent), the use of the perfect basin forecast method would improve upon climatology in only five of the subsequent nine years, indistinguishable from chance.[4] Because overall basin activity predictions are not perfect, this is the idealized best case scenario.

To summarize, over periods less than a decade (perhaps even several decades), and certainly on the timescale of years, the total number of named storms offers little if any advantage over climatology for anticipating landfalling hurricanes. There are three main reasons for this conclusion. First, even though landfall proportions cannot be shown to have changed since at least

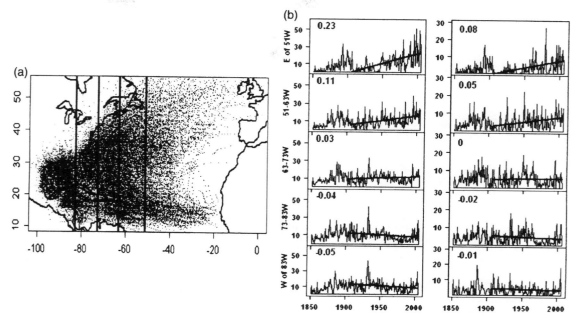

FIGURE 4 (a) NATL basin divided into five quintiles, each with an equal number of observations from the HURDAT dataset. (b) Measures of activity in each quartile: total number of storm days (left panel) and total number of hurricane days (right panel); trends are computed and shown (upper left, best fit line) from 1900

Source: Figures provided courtesy of S. McIntyre.

1950, the extremely large variability in this metric alone (see Figure 3) complicates any prediction of landfall based on first predicting the overall basin activity. Second, changes observed in the overall basin activity are not spatially uniform; increasing activity has occurred far from land. Finally, because the skill of existing seasonal predictions of basin activity is modest at best (e.g. Owens and Landsea, 2003), efforts to predict landfall rates on longer timescales based on NATL basin activity are unlikely to be forthcoming in the near term. Practically useful forecasts of landfall at timescales of one to five years will require the use of variables other than the number of storms in the basin.

3.4. El Niño: Southern Oscillation and landfall

Because there is no simple way either to predict overall basin activity or its annual relationship with landfalling hurricanes, scientists have looked for ways to explain the patterns of variability in storm activity. Many of such studies focus on NATL basin activity, but some also focus on landfalling hurricanes. The most well documented and strongest relationship is that between the El Niño-Southern Oscillation (ENSO, measured via the Southern Oscillation Index or temperatures of the equatorial Pacific Ocean) and storm landfalls.

Figure 5 shows the number of US hurricane landfalls in different states of ENSO from 1950 to 2007. Over this period there were fewer hurricane landfalls during El Niño years than during La Niña years.

Pielke and Landsea (1999) showed a relationship between ENSO and normalized damages (cf. Katz, 2002), and this relationship continues to hold through 2008 as shown in Table 4. Predictability of the state of ENSO shows skill only on timescales of less than a year, and even then the skill is not particularly large (Camargo et al., 2007). Thus, while ENSO has a significant

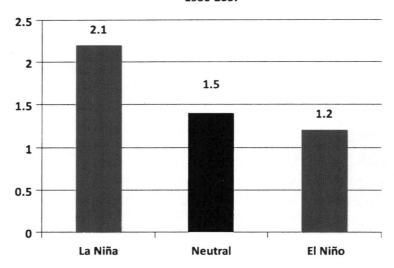

FIGURE 5 Average US landfalls by state of ENSO, 1950–2007. The SST data is from the NOAA Climate Prediction Center and is a three-month running mean for August, September and October of ERSST.v3 SST anomalies in the Niño 3.4 region (i.e. 5° N–5° S, 120°–170° W); available at www.cpc.noaa.gov/products/analysis_monitoring/ensostuff/ensoyears.shtml. An El Niño year is defined by NOAA as an anomaly of 0.5°C or larger and a La Niña year is defined by an anomaly of –0.5°C or less. From 1950 to 2007 there were 18 La Niña years, 22 neutral years and 18 El Niño years

relationship with landfalls and damage, the ability to skilfully predict ENSO events more than a season or two in advance limits its use as a guide to landfalls and damages on a timescale of one to five years, leading scientists to explore other relationships.

3.5. Sea surface temperatures, climate oscillations, solar cycles and more

Scientists have published widely on the relationships of hurricane activity and sea surface temperatures (SSTs), Pacific Decadal Oscillation (PDO), North Atlantic Oscillation (NAO), Atlantic Multidecadal Oscillation (AMO), Atlantic Multi-decadal Mode (AMM) and even more exotic relationships such as with the Quasibiennial Oscillation (QBO), Cold Tongue Index (CTI), African dust and rainfall, Asian and North American smog, sunspot activity and more. Some of this literature was reviewed by an international working group of the World Meteorological Organization (World Meteorological Organization, 2006; more recently, see Bogen et al., 2007).

Other studies have been developed by researchers at Florida State University, seeking to identify relationships of ENSO, NAO and AMO on landfalling storms and damage (e.g. Elsner and Jagger, 2006; Jagger et al., 2008). Elsner and Jagger (2008) find a relationship between the solar cycle and US hurricane counts, after accounting for SSTs, wind shear and steering currents.

Saunders and Lea (2005) use a metric of tropospheric winds to develop a model of landfalling activity, which its lead author characterized as

TABLE 4 Replication of Table 2 in Pielke and Landsea (1999) using updated statistics on normalized damage and ENSO (including 2007)

	Median damage (USD billion)	Mean damage (USD billion)	Std dev (USD billion)
La Niña	6.6	9.2	10.5
Neutral	0.4	12.7	30.4
El Niño	0.4	7.7	14.5

'the first to offer precision which is high enough to be practically useful' (Saunders, 2005).[5] The methodology was used subsequently in 2006–2008, resulting in a prediction issued each August for the current hurricane season, and in each case predicting landfall numbers to be above average. For these three years the number of landfalls was well below the historical mean in 2006 and 2007 and above average in 2008 (TSR, 2009). In stark contrast, Swanson (2008) suggests that the relationship between atmospheric winds and hurricane activity is in fact in the opposite direction, with the hurricanes perturbing the wind fields. Regardless of the direction of causality, there is no evidence that atmospheric winds can be predicted on timescales of a year or more.

The very public and sometimes acrimonious debate over climate change includes some who posit a straightforward relationship between increasing SSTs and increasing storm activity (e.g. Holland and Webster, 2007). If there is such a simple relationship, then increasing SSTs would be accompanied by increasing storm activity, landfalls and damage. Others have suggested a much more complicated relationship, even leading to suggestions of decreasing storm counts in the NATL (e.g. Emanuel et al., 2008; Knutson et al., 2008). Vecchi et al. (2008) show how different, legitimate views on the science lead to vastly different projections for future NATL activity. Presently, and indeed for the foreseeable future, debate over the effects of climate change on hurricane activity will remain contested (Pielke et al., 2005).

Risk Management Solutions (RMS) Ltd, a leading catastrophe modelling firm, has used a range of models coupled with expert elicitation to develop five-year forecasts of US hurricane landfall activity that it utilizes in its models used widely in the insurance and reinsurance industries (Lonfat et al., 2007; Jewson et al., 2009).[6] The RMS methodology resulted in an estimated 2.1 landfalling hurricanes and 0.9 landfalling intense hurricanes each year from 2006 to 2010. The actual values for 2006–2008 (i.e. the first three years of the forecast) are 1.3

hurricane landfalls and zero landfalling intense hurricanes per year. The long-term climatology would have suggested 1.5 hurricane landfalls and about 0.6 intense hurricane landfalls. To improve upon climatology for the five-year period of the forecast would require seven hurricane landfalls in 2009 and 2010, five of which are intense hurricanes.[7] The RMS estimates have been controversial because when incorporated into their catastrophe model as a 'short-term' outlook on activity, they lead directly to increased insurance rates, with corresponding financial benefits for many of the clients of RMS (see Hunter and Birnbaum, 2006).

Although much has been learned about tropical cyclones and various modes of climate, none has thus far resulted in knowledge that has been shown to provide skilful predictions of out-of-sample (i.e. in real time) US landfalls or damage on timescales of one to five years (cf. Karen Clark and Company, 2008). One reason for this is that the track record of such forecasts is not long. However, the experience that is available to date does not suggest optimism. Even so, those who may differ with the conclusions reached here can support their view by issuing predictions shown to be skilful on timescales of one to five years, and sustain accurate enough performance over time to show skill. But demonstrating such skill will probably impossible for at least several decades, and the next section explains why this is so.

4. The impossibility of demonstrating skilful predictive capabilities in the near term, or how the guaranteed winner scam meets the hot hand fallacy

Upon seeing efforts to establish relationships between various climate variables and NATL hurricane activity one is tempted to quote John von Neumann who said of fitting relationships with various parameters, 'with four parameters I can fit an elephant, and with five I can make him wiggle his trunk' (as related in Dyson, 2004). Indeed, my own research shows a correlation of

0.33 between the total score in the UK Football Association's (FA's) annual Cup Championship game and the subsequent hurricane season's damage, without even controlling for SSTs, ENSO or the Premier League tables. Years in which the FA Cup championship game has a total of three or more goals have an average of 1.8 landfalling hurricanes and USD11.7 billion in damage, whereas championships with a total of one or two goals have had an average of only 1.3 storms and USD6.7 billion in damage.

I am sure that no one would believe that there is a causal relationship between FA Cup championship game scores and US hurricane landfalls, yet the existence of a spurious relationship should provide a reason for caution when interpreting far more plausible relationships. Two simple dynamics associated with interpreting predictions help to explain why fundamental uncertainties in hurricane landfalls will inevitably persist.

The first of these dynamics is what might be called the 'guaranteed winner scam'. It works like this: select 65,536 people and tell them that you have developed a methodology that allows for 100 per cent accurate prediction of the winner of next weekend's big football game. You split the group of 65,536 into equal halves and send one half a guaranteed prediction of victory for one team, and the other half a guaranteed win on the other team. You have ensured that your prediction will be viewed as correct by 32,768 people. Each week you can proceed in this fashion. By the time eight weeks have gone by there will be 256 people anxiously waiting for your next week's selection because you have demonstrated remarkable predictive capabilities, having provided them with eight perfect picks. Presumably they will now be ready to pay a handsome price for the predictions you offer in week nine.

Now instead of predictions of football match winners, think of real-time predictions of hurricane landfall and activity. The diversity of available predictions exceeds the range of observed landfall behaviour. Consider, for example, Jewson et al. (2009) which presents a suite of 20 different models that lead to predictions of

2007–2012 landfall activity to be from more than 8 per cent below the 1900–2006 mean to 43 per cent above that mean, with 18 values falling in between. Over the next five years it is virtually certain that one or more of these models will have provided a prediction that will be more accurate than the long-term historical baseline (i.e. will be skilful). A broader review of the literature beyond this one paper would show an even wider range of predictions. The user of these predictions has no way of knowing whether the skill was the result of true predictive skill or just chance, given a very wide range of available predictions. And because the scientific community is constantly introducing new methods of prediction the 'guaranteed winner scam' can go on forever with little hope for certainty.[8]

Complicating the issue is the 'hot hand fallacy' which was coined to describe how people misinterpret random sequences, based on how they view the tendency of basketball players to be 'streak shooters' or have the 'hot hand' (Gilovich et al., 1985). The 'hot hand fallacy' holds that the probability in a random process of a 'hit' (i.e. a made basket or a successful hurricane landfall forecast) is higher after a 'hit' than the baseline probability.[9] In other words, people often see patterns in random signals that they then use, incorrectly, to ascribe information about the future.

The 'hot hand fallacy' can manifest itself in several ways with respect to hurricane landfall forecasts. First, the wide range of available predictions essentially spanning the range of possibilities means that some predictions for the next years will be shown to have been skilful. Even if the skill is the result of the comprehensive randomness of the 'guaranteed winner scam' there will be a tendency for people to gravitate to that particular predictive methodology for future forecasts. Second, a defining feature of climatology is persistence, suggesting that nature does sometimes have a 'hot hand'. However, this too can lead one astray. Consider that following the record number of landfalls and damage of 2004 and 2005, global hurricane activity dropped to extremely low levels (Maue, 2009). Distinguishing between a true 'hot hand' and a 'winner's scam' can only occur over a period substantially longer than the timescales of prediction.

As a result of these dynamics, robust predictive skill can be shown only over the fairly long term, offering real-time predictions and carefully evaluating their performance. The necessary time period is many decades. Judgements of skilful predictive methodologies on shorter time-scales must be based on guesswork or other factors beyond empirical information on predictive performance.

5. Conclusion: What is a decision maker to do?

This paper has argued that efforts to develop skilful predictions of landfalling hurricanes or damage on timescales of one to five years have shown no success. It has further argued that, given the diversity of predictions now available on these timescales, inevitably some will appear skilful in coming years. However, despite the tendency to view these predictions as actually skilful, a much longer perspective than the timescale of the predictions will be needed to robustly evaluate their performance. This sets up a frustrating situation where decision making must be made under conditions of irreducible uncertainty and ignorance.

So what might a decision maker concerned about hurricane landfalls or damage over the next one to five years actually do?

The recommendation here is to start with the historical data as a starting point for judging the likelihood of future events and their impacts. Figure 6 shows the frequency of landfalling hurricanes per year for the period 1851–2008 (other time periods are shown in Table 2, and decision makers may wish to use a record that starts in 1900 for data quality reasons). Similarly, Figure 7 shows the same data but for running five-year periods from 1851 to 2008.

A decision maker may have reasons to hedge his or her views of these distributions in one way or another, and (s)he will certainly be able to find a scientific justification for whatever hedge (s)he prefers (see Murphy, 1978).

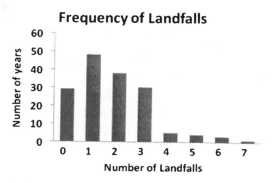

FIGURE 6 Histogram of annual number of landfalls, 1851–2008

However, it is important to recognize that any decision to adjust expectations away from those in the historical record represents a hedge. Reasons for hedging might include risk aversion or risk-seeking behaviour, a gut feeling, trust in a subset of the expert community, a need to justify decisions made for other reasons and so on. But at present, there is no single, shared *scientific* justification for altering expectations away from the historical record. There are instead many scientific justifications pointing in different directions.

Starting with the historical record allows for a clear and unambiguous identification of hedging strategies and justifications for them. An ability to distinguish between judgements that can be made based on empirical analysis and those that are based on speculation or selectivity is an important factor in using science in decision making. Such a distinction can also help to identify the role that financial or other

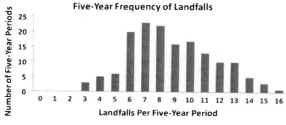

FIGURE 7 Histogram of running five-year number of landfalls, 1851–2008

interests play in the choice of relevant science in a particular decision process.

Given that the climate system is known to be non-stationary on various timescales, there are of course good reasons to expect that uncertainties may be larger than the variability observed in the past, given that the climate system can assume modes of behaviour not observed over the past century and a half. Each decision maker should carefully evaluate how *unknown unknowns* might influence their judgements. In addition to decision making under conditions of uncertainty, decision makers need also to make judgements under conditions of ignorance, where uncertainties cannot be known with certainty.

Decision makers will continue to make bets on the future and, just like in a casino, some bets will prove winners and some will be losers. But over the long term those who do the best in the business of decision making related to hurricane landfalls and their impacts will be those who best match their decisions to what can and cannot be known about the uncertain future. And such wisdom starts with understanding the historical record and why the scientific community cannot produce skilful forecasts of future landfalls and damage for the foreseeable future.

Acknowledgements

Useful comments and suggestions were received from Chris Austin, Joel Gratz, Iris Grossman, Mark Jelinek, Jan Kleinn, Phil Klotzbach, Pete Kozich, Steve McIntyre, Rade Musulin, Roger Pielke, Sr, Silvio Schmidt, Mohan Sharma, David Smith and William Travis. Special thanks to Daniel Hawallek, Leonard Smith and Jianming Yin for independent checks of data and analysis. All responsibility for the paper lies with the author.

Notes

1. The choice of dataset does not influence the results presented here, as the two methods lead to very similar results. The data used here express losses in constant 2008 US dollars, under the assumption that loss potentials plus inflation have increased by 4 per cent per year since 2005, leading to a 12.5 per cent increase in the normalized data from the 2005 baseline. 2006 had no hurricane landfalls, and thus no damage. 2007 had one landfall, with USD500 million in damage (see Blake, 2007). 2008 had three hurricane landfalls with an estimated USD16.6 billion in total losses, made by doubling the estimates of onshore insured losses provided by the Insurance Services Office for Louisiana and Texas in the third quarter of 2008 (see Insurance Services Office, 2008).
2. See www.aoml.noaa.gov/hrd/hurdat/Data_Storm. html.
3. All correlations with damage are expressed using the rank (Spearman) correlation.
4. This conclusion is identical using data from 1966, the start of the geostationary satellite era.
5. A team of researchers at Colorado State University has also issued landfall forecasts in recent years (see CSU, 2009).
6. This author participated in the 2008 elicitation process.
7. Because RMS issues a new five-year forecast each year, they are now in the interesting situation where the most recent five-year forecast is inconsistent with the one issued from 2006–2010 as they imply different rates of occurrence for the period of overlap.
8. What if the nature of relationships and processes in the global atmosphere is non-stationary on timescales less than that required to demonstrate skill with certainty? See Pielke (2009) for a discussion.
9. The 'gambler's fallacy' is also relevant here. It posits that the odds of a miss are higher after a run of 'hits'.

References

Blake, E. S., 2007. *Tropical Cyclone Report: Hurricane Humberto*. National Hurricane Center, 28 November. www. nhc.noaa.gov/pdf/TCR-AL092007_Humberto.pdf.

Bogen, K. T., Jones, E. D. and Fischer, L. E., 2007. Hurricane destructive power predictions based on historical storm and sea surface temperature data. *Risk Analysis*, 27. 1497–1517.

Briggs, W., 2008. On the changes in the number and intensity of North Atlantic tropical cyclones. *Journal of Climate*, 21. 1387–1402.

Camargo, S. J., Barnston, A. G., Klotzbach, P. J. and Landsea, C. W., 2007. Seasonal tropical cyclone forecasts. *WMO Bulletin*, 56. 297–309.

Coughlin, K., Bellone, E., Laepple, T., Jewson, S. and Nzerem, K., 2009. A relationship between all Atlantic hurricanes and those that make landfall in the USA. *Quarterly Journal of the Royal Meteorological Society*, 135. 371–379.

CSU, 2009. *The Tropical Meteorology Project.* Colorado State University, Fort Collins, CO. http://typhoon.atmos.colostate.edu/forecasts.

Dyson, F., 2004. A meeting with Enrico Fermi. *Nature*, 427. 297.

Elsner, J. B. and Bossack, B. H., 2001. Bayesian analysis of US hurricane climate. *Journal of Climate*, 14. 4341–4350.

Elsner, J. and Jagger, T., 2006. Prediction models for annual US hurricane counts. *Journal of Climate*, 19. 2935–2952.

Elsner, J. and Jagger, T., 2008. United States and Caribbean tropical cyclone activity related to the solar cycle. *Geophysical Research Letters*, 35. L18705. doi:10.1029/2008/GL034431.

Elsner, J., Niu, X. and Jagger, T., 2003. Detecting shifts in hurricane rates using a Markov Chain Monte Carlo approach. *Journal of Climate*, 17. 2652–2666.

Emanuel, K., 2005. Emanuel replies. *Nature*, 438. doi:10.1038/nature04427.

Emanuel, K., Sundararajan, R. and William, J., 2008. Hurricanes and global warming: results from downscaling IPCC AR4 simulations. *Journal of Climate*, 89. 347–367.

Gilovich, T., Vallone, R. and Tversky, A., 1985. The hot hand in basketball: on the misperception of random sequences. *Cognitive Psychology*, 17. 295–314.

Holland, G. J. and Webster, P. J., 2007. Heightened tropical cyclone activity in the North Atlantic: natural variability or climate trend? *Philosophical Transactions of the Royal Society* doi:10.1098/rsta. 2007.2083.

Hunter, J. R. and Birnbaum, B., 2006. Letter to the Honorable Alessandro Iuppa, NAIC President, Superintendent, Maine Bureau of Insurance, 27 March. www.consumerfed.org/pdfs/Insurance_NAIC_RMS_Letter_032706.pdf.

Insurance Services Office, 2008. Insurers to pay $11.5 billion in third-quarter catastrophe claims, says ISO's Property Claim Services Unit. www.iso.com/Press-Releases/2008/Insurers-to-Pay-$11.5-Billion-in-Third-Quarter-Catastrophe-Claims-Says-ISOs-Property-Claim-Service.html.

Jagger, T., Elsner, J. and Saunders, M., 2008. Forecasting US insured hurricane losses. *Climate Extremes and Society*, H.F. Diaz (ed). Cambridge University Press, Cambridge, UK. 189–208.

Jewson, S., Bellone, E., Khare, S., Laepple, T., Lonfat, M., Nzerem, K., O'Shay, A., Penzer, J. and Coughlin, K.,

2009. 5 year prediction of the number of hurricanes which make US landfall. *Hurricanes and Climate Change*, J. B. Elsner and T. H. Jagger (eds). Springer-Verlag, New York, NY.

Karen Clark and Company, 2008. *Near Term Hurricane Models: How Have They Performed?* www.karenclarkandco.com/home/page/newsPress.aspx#pressReleases20091216.

Katz, R. W., 2002. Stochastic modeling of hurricane damage. *Journal of Applied Meteorology*, 41. 754–762.

Knutson, T. R., Sirutis, J. J., Garner, S. T., Vecchi, G. A. and Held, I. M., 2008. Simulated reduction in Atlantic hurricane frequency under twenty-first-century warming conditions. *Nature Geoscience*, 1. 359–364.

Landsea, C. W., 2005. Hurricanes and global warming. *Nature*, 438. doi:10.1038/nature04477.

Landsea, C. W., 2007. Counting Atlantic Tropical Cyclones back to 1900. *EOS*, 88. 197 and 202.

Lonfat, M., Boissonnade, A. and Muir-Wood, R., 2007. Atlantic Basin, US and Caribbean landfall rates over the 2006–2010 period: an insurance industry perspective. *Tellus A*, 59. 499–510.

Lu, Y. and Garrido, J., 2005. Doubly periodic non-homogeneous Poisson models for hurricane data. *Statistical Methodology*, 2. 17–35.

Maue, R. N., 2009. Northern Hemisphere Tropical Cyclone activity. *Geophysical Research Letters*, March. www.agu.org/pubs/crossref/2009/2008GL035946.shtml.

Murphy, A. H., 1978. Hedging and the mode of expression in weather forecasts. *Bulletin of the American Meteorological Society*, 59. 371–373.

Nzerem, K., Jewson, S. and Laepple, K., 2008. Change-point detection in the historical hurricane number time-series: why can't we detect change-points at US landfall? arXiv:physics/0611107v1 *[physics.ao-ph]*, 2 February. http://arxiv.org/PS_cache/physics/pdf/0611/0611107v1.pdf.

Owens, B. F. and Landsea, C. W., 2003. Assessing the skill of operational Atlantic seasonal tropical cyclone forecasts. *Weather and Forecasting*, 18. 45–54.

Pielke, R. A. Jr, 2005. Hurricanes and global warming. *Nature*, 438. doi:10.1038/nature04426.

Pielke, R. A. Jr, 2009. Collateral damage in the death of stationarity. *GEWEX Newsletter*. May. 5–7. www.gewex.org/images/may2009.pdf.

Pielke, R. A. Jr and Landsea, C. W., 1998. Normalized hurricane damages in the United States: 1925–95. *Weather and Forecasting*, American Meteorological Society. 621–631.

Pielke, R. A. Jr and Landsea, C. W., 1999. La Niña, El Niño, and Atlantic Hurricane Damages in the

United States. *Bulletin of the American Meteorological Society*, 80. 2027–2033.

Pielke, R. A. Jr and McIntyre, S., 2007. *Changes in Spatial Distribution of North Atlantic Tropical Cyclones, NG31A-07.* Annual Meeting of the American Geophysical Union, December. www.climateaudit.org/pdf/agu07.hurricane.ppt.

Pielke, R. A. Jr, Landsea, C., Mayfield, M., Laver, J. and Pasch, R., 2005. Hurricanes and global warming. *Bulletin of the American Meteorological Society*, 86. 1571–1575.

Pielke, R. A. Jr, Hoeppe, P. and McIntyre, S., 2008. Case studies in disaster losses and climate change. *Proceedings of the 15th 'Aha Huliko' a Winter Workshop on Extreme Events.* University of Hawaii, Honolulu, January. 131–140.

Saunders, M. A., 2005. Breakthrough in hurricane prediction. *UCL Science*, 19. 8–9.

Saunders, M. A. and Lea, A. S., 2005. Seasonal prediction of hurricane activity reaching the coast of the United States. *Nature*, 434. 1005–1008.

Smith, R. L., 2008. Statistical trend analysis in weather and climate extremes in a changing climate. Regions of focus: North America, Hawaii, Caribbean, and US Pacific Islands. *A Report by the US Climate Change Science Program and the Subcommittee on Global Change Research*, T. R. Karl, G. A. Meehl, C. D. Miller, , S. J. Hassol, A. M. Waple and W. L. Murray (eds). US Climate Change Science Program, Washington, DC.

Solow, A. R. and Moore, L., 2002. Testing for trend in North Atlantic hurricane activity, 1900–98. *Journal of Climate*, 15. 3111–3114.

Swanson, K., 2008. False causality between Atlantic hurricane activity fluctuations and seasonal lower atmospheric wind anomalies. *Geophysical Research Letters*, 35. L18807. doi:10.1029/2008GL034469.

TSR, 2009. *Tropical Storm Risk*, researched and developed by M. Saunders, F. Roberts and A. Lea. University College, London. www.tropicalstormrisk.com.

Vecchi, G., Swanson, K. L. and Soden, B. J., 2008. Wither hurricane activity? *Science*, 322. 687–689.

World Meteorological Organization, 2006. *Statement on Tropical Cyclones and Climate Change.* WMO Tropical Meteorology Research Programme Committee TC2: Impact of Climate Change on Tropical Cyclones. www.wmo.int/pages/prog/arep/tmrp/documents/iwtc_statement.pdf.

ENVIRONMENTAL HAZARDS
Human and Policy Dimensions

Building a low-carbon economy: The inaugural report of the UK Committee on Climate Change

SAMUEL FANKHAUSER[1,*], DAVID KENNEDY[2] AND JIM SKEA[3]

[1]Grantham Research Institute and Centre for Climate Change Economics and Policy, London School of Economics, Houghton Street, London WC2A 2AE
[2]Committee on Climate Change, Manning House, 22 Carlisle Place, London SW1P 1JA
[3]UK Energy Research Centre, 58 Princes Gate, Exhibition Road, London SW7 2PG

The 2008 Climate Change Act commits the UK to a legally binding emissions target for 2050. The Act also puts in place a new institutional architecture to ensure this long-term objective is achieved. UK emissions will be controlled through a series of statutory five-year carbon budgets, the first three of which were set in Spring 2009. Recommending the targets and overseeing compliance with them is a new independent body, the Committee on Climate Change (CCC). This paper summarizes the inaugural report of the CCC, published in December 2008, and explains the analytical basis behind its recommendations: a long-term reduction in all greenhouse gas emissions of at least 80 per cent, relative to 1990, by 2050, and an initial cut in emissions of 34 per cent over the first three budgets (2008–2022), potentially rising to 42 per cent in the context of a new international agreement post-2012.

Keywords: climate change risks; GHG mitigation; UK climate policy

1. Background

Climate change is arguably the biggest environmental hazard of our time. It is also one of the most difficult environmental problems to solve. Tackling climate change requires an unprecedented level of global environmental cooperation and a sustained, multi-decade commitment to the decarbonization of the economy. The technological and economic solutions of doing so are emerging, but maintaining a long-term, global commitment is difficult institutionally in national systems geared toward the short and medium term.

In November 2008 the British Parliament passed a progressive piece of legislation which may help to overcome this problem in the UK. The Climate Change Act, which had overwhelming support from all political parties, breaks new institutional ground in at least three respects.

First, it sets a legally binding long-term emissions target. The Act obliges the UK to reduce its greenhouse gas emissions by at least 80 per cent by 2050. Many policy makers have advocated such long-term targets, not least the leaders of the G8 nations at their 2009 summit. However, the UK is the first country to put the commitment into law.

Second, the Act puts into place a framework through which the long-term target will be achieved. It commits the UK to a series of legally binding five-year carbon budgets leading towards the long-term goal. The purpose of the budgets is to provide a clear benchmark against which the country's emissions performance can be measured and tracked. The budgets also send a strong signal to investors about the UK's carbon policy, which should facilitate low-carbon investment and help to reduce regulatory uncertainty.

■ *Corresponding author. *E-mail:* **s.fankhauser@lse.ac.uk**

ENVIRONMENTAL HAZARDS **8 (2009) 201–208**

doi:10.3763/ehaz.2009.0020 © 2009 Earthscan ISSN: 1747-7891 (print), 1878-0059 (online) www.earthscanjournals.com

Budgets are set sufficiently far in advance to provide medium-term certainty without reducing the scope for mid-term corrections. The first three budgets covering the period 2008–2022, for example, were announced in April 2009. The five-year time horizon is thought to be long enough to absorb short-term fluctuations in emissions, for example due to weather extremes or variations in the business cycle.

Third, the Climate Change Act establishes a new independent body, the Committee on Climate Change (CCC), which advises the government on carbon budgets and monitors progress in meeting them in an annual report to government. Applying a transparent, evidence-based approach to setting and meeting budgets, the CCC is intended to support the development of robust carbon strategies and increase the likelihood of meeting the ambitious emissions reduction targets it helps to set. The legal framework requires the discussion of CCC advice and of its annual progress reports in Parliament. This lends the CCC considerable leverage to hold the government to account.

The CCC, which had been active in shadow-form since February 2008, issued its first set of recommendations in October 2008, when it advocated a long-term emissions reduction objective for the UK of 80 per cent, relative to 1990, and the extension of the target to all greenhouse gases, not just CO_2. These recommendations were subsequently adopted and incorporated in the Climate Change Act.

In December 2008, the Committee published its first full report (CCC, 2008), which elaborates on the reasoning behind the 80 per cent recommendation and proposes emissions targets for the first three carbon budgets (2008–2012, 2013–2017 and 2018–2022). It recommends that by 2020 UK greenhouse gas emissions should come down by 42 per cent as part of a stringent international agreement that builds on the current Kyoto commitments. Until such an agreement is reached the UK should commit to a 34 per cent unilateral cut.

The report also discusses a number of additional issues, such as the role of international carbon trading and the wider social and economic consequences of the proposed targets, including the likely cost to the economy, the impact on competitiveness and fuel poverty, the effect on energy security, fiscal implications and the consequences for the devolved administrations.

This paper provides a summary of the CCC's inaugural report, which centred on the appropriate medium- and long-term targets to contain climate change risks, and discusses the analytical underpinnings of its recommendations. The focus is on the two main recommendations of the report: the target for 2050, discussed in Section 2, and the first three carbon budgets, discussed in Section 3. The final section outlines the CCC's future work programme.

2. The UK's long-term target (2050)

The Climate Change Act was not the first policy document to propose a long-term emissions target for the UK (although it was the first to put it into law). In 2000 the Royal Commission on Environmental Pollution (RCEP, 2000) had recommended a 60 per cent reduction target for CO_2 only. This number was subsequently adopted in the 2003 Energy White Paper (DTI, 2003). The 60 per cent number also featured as a minimum requirement in early drafts of what eventually became the Climate Change Act.

In the event, the Act adopted, at the recommendation of the CCC, a much tighter and also broader target. The 2050 reduction target was increased from 60 per cent to at least 80 per cent and the scope was extended to cover not only CO_2 but the full basket of Kyoto greenhouse gases (CO_2, CH_4, N_2O, HFCs, PFCs and SF_6).

The target applies to the economy as a whole and not to individual sectors or gases. That is, it is possible for some sectors to remain above the overall target as long as this is compensated for by additional reductions elsewhere.

The inclusion of all Kyoto gases in the target was a fairly uncontroversial adjustment that underlines the importance of controlling all

10

greenhouse gases. In the same spirit the target was extended to also include the international transport sector (aviation and shipping). The only reason to exclude some activities would have been measurement and accounting issues. Although these are valid, particularly in the case of international transport, the CCC felt that they can and should be overcome before 2050.[1]

The switch from a 60 to 80 per cent target reflects two important developments since the Royal Commission issued its recommendation. The first is an increased concern among scientists about the speed and severity of climate change. The faster-than-expected pace of observed climate change, a better understanding of feedback effects and a greater awareness of potentially abrupt or irreversible change have led to a re-evaluation of climate change risks (see Solomon et al., 2007).

The second development is that global emissions and atmospheric concentration levels have grown faster than anticipated a few years ago. An important factor in this trend has been the rapid economic development in countries like China and India, whose emissions have grown much faster than expected. The accelerated growth in concentrations – even if it slows temporarily as a result of the current economic crisis – means measures to reduce emissions have to be brought forward.

In devising its recommended target, the CCC worked backwards, first defining an acceptable global temperature goal, then calculating emissions trajectories consistent with that goal and finally setting the UK's contribution to the global trajectory. The process was strongly evidence-based and made extensive use of model results, but it was not an integrated, model-based optimization. The recommendations are ultimately judgemental.

There is an intensive and ongoing debate about the globally optimal greenhouse gas emissions trajectory, and the different points of view are backed up by a variety of economic, ethical and environmental arguments. The Intergovernmental Panel on Climate Change (IPCC), for example, distinguishes five 'reasons for concern', which all imply different climate policies. They include concern about aggregate economic impacts, the unfair distribution of these impacts, the threat to unique natural systems, the danger of passing irreversible impact thresholds and the costs associated with increased climate variability (Smith et al., 2001; 2009).

The CCC considered these approaches and in particular studied carefully the lessons from integrated assessment models (Sura and Golborne, 2008) and the Stern Review (Dietz, 2008). In the end it decided on a risk-based approach, arguing that climate policy is ultimately an issue of risk and that there is still too much uncertainty in climate models to set precise policy targets.

The CCC adopted two benchmark objectives. The first was to keep the central warming projection (mode) as close as possible to 2°C above the 1990–2000 average. Although 2°C is not a firm threshold it was felt that the global danger zone will start somewhere above 2°C. The second benchmark was to minimize the risk of a catastrophic outcome. This latter objective was specified to mean a less than 1 per cent probability of surpassing 4°C. These benchmarks will be reviewed as the science evolves, for example when setting the fourth carbon budget (2023–2027) at the end of 2010. Setting targets is an 'act-learn-react' process.

The MAGICC model[2] was then used to derive emission trajectories consistent with this goal. The model runs suggested that, to have a reasonable chance of meeting the two objectives, global emissions would have to peak within the next decade or so and then decline by at least 3 per cent annually. This result is broadly consistent with the literature (e.g. Meinshausen et al., 2006).

The final step was to decide on the UK's contribution to the global trajectory. A wide range of burden-sharing arguments have been put forward in the literature, some emphasizing per capita emissions (e.g. contraction and convergence), others the carbon efficiency of an economy (e.g. triptych), but all based broadly on the UNFCCC principle of 'common but differentiated responsibilities' (see the discussion in CCC, 2008).

The CCC did not make an ethical choice between those methods. Instead it argued pragmatically that it is difficult to imagine a global deal that would not ask developed countries to reduce their per capita emissions to global average levels. Allowing some large emitters to remain above the global average would require other emitters to remain below it, and agreement on such an outcome is unlikely.

This argumentation, first put forward by Stern (2008), implies a roughly 80 per cent reduction in UK emissions from currently just over 10 tCO_2e per capita to around 2–2.5 tCO_2e per capita. In absolute terms, the UK would have to reduce emissions from 695 $MtCO_2e$ in 2006 to 159 $MtCO_2e$ in 2050 (see Figure 1). The 80 per cent target is in line with a growing international consensus on, and commitment to, long-term emission cuts by developed countries. The target is formulated as a minimum requirement, leaving open the option of further cuts if required (for example in the light of new scientific evidence).

Despite framing climate change as a risk issue, the CCC did not ignore the issue of mitigation costs, which is central to economic assessments. Considerable effort went into ascertaining that

the proposed targets are technically feasible and can be achieved at reasonable cost. They can. The CCC's modelling results, based on MARKAL, concur with the IPCC fourth assessment (Barker et al., 2007) that cutting emissions by four-fifths would cost no more than 1–2 per cent of GDP in 2050 (see AEA, 2008).

A key plank of the long-term abatement strategy would have to be the decarbonization of the electricity sector, through a combination of renewable energy, nuclear power and carbon capture and sequestration (CCS). On the back of a decarbonized electricity sector, large-scale emission reductions would also become feasible in two other important sectors, heating and transport. In the short term, significant contributions would have to come from increased energy efficiency in buildings, transport and industry. Although it endorsed the free trade in carbon emissions, the CCC also noted that the majority of the 80 per cent cut would in the long term have to be achieved via domestic action.

3. The first three carbon budgets (2008–2022)

The introduction of five-year carbon budgets is arguably the key institutional innovation of the Climate Change Act. From a political economy point of view, the budgets allay concerns that without intermediate milestones action toward the mid-century target would be delayed and they allow for the objective and transparent monitoring of performance. The budgets also increase policy certainty and send a strong signal to industry, encouraging business to undertake the large-scale investments needed to create a low-carbon economy.

Each carbon budget constitutes a distinct five-year target. However, the CCC used the year 2020, the mid-point of the third budget period, to take a 'sighting shot' at appropriate budgets for periods one to three. The CCC recommended a two-track approach with two state-contingent targets (see Figure 2):

■ An *interim target* of −34 per cent, relative to 1990, to which the UK should commit unilaterally; and

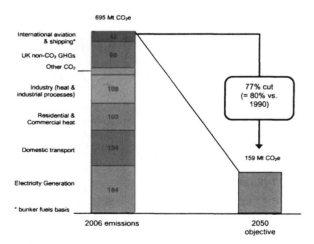

FIGURE 1 Current UK emissions and the 2050 target
Source: CCC (2008).
Note: UK emissions in 2006 (including transport) were 16% lower than in 1990. Hence an 80% emissions cut relative to 1990 translates into a $(1 - 0.20/0.84) = 77\%$ reduction from today.

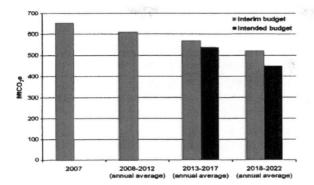

FIGURE 2 CCC recommendation for the 2008–2022 carbon budgets
Source: CCC (2008).

■ An *intended target* of −42 per cent, relative to 1990, which the UK should adopt if a meaningful successor to the Kyoto Protocol can be agreed.

Consistent with the long-term target, the carbon budgets cover all Kyoto gases, despite uncertainty in the measurement of non-CO$_2$ emissions, particularly in agriculture. However, the CCC recommended the exclusion of emissions from international aviation and shipping until a transparent and sensible way could be found to allocate international emissions to the national level. The CCC recognized the importance of international transport emissions, however, and will monitor them in its annual progress reports. It also argued that the level of ambition in the budgets should reflect likely progress in reducing emissions in these sectors.

In recommending the three carbon budgets the CCC was guided by three main concerns: (1) the need for consistency with EU-wide energy and climate change policy, (2) the need to be consistent with the 2050 objective and make an adequate early contribution to the 2050 target; and (3) the need for budgets that are ambitious but technically and economically feasible.

The distinction between an interim and intended budget was a direct result of EU policy approach, which also distinguishes a 'unilateral' target (a 20 per cent EU-wide emissions cut) and

a 'global cooperation' target (a 30 per cent emissions cut). The CCC felt this was an appropriate way to approach the international negotiations for a post-2012 agreement. The targets proposed for the UK are roughly consistent with the obligations that the EU-internal burden sharing methodology imposes on the UK.

Similarly, the budgets set the UK on course to reach its 2050 target. Meeting the intended budget target would require a decrease in UK greenhouse gas emissions of 2.8 per cent per annum between 2007 and 2020. This would have to increase to 3.5 per cent per annum between 2020 and 2050. Although the initial reduction rate is lower than the long-term average, the CCC felt it was adequate. In an environment of high uncertainty, the proposed targets also provide the flexibility required to make cost-effective mid-term corrections should new information become available (Watkiss et al., 2008).

Although consistency with EU policies and the long-term target is crucial, by far the most effort went into the third consideration – ascertaining that the proposed targets are technically and economically feasible. The CCC systematically assessed the emission reduction potential in the main sectors – electric power, transport, buildings and industry, and the non-CO$_2$ sectors.

Detailed marginal abatement cost curves were derived for all relevant sectors to identify emission reduction opportunities through a bottom-up process. About half of the UK's emissions are covered by the EU Emissions Trading Scheme (ETS). The CCC estimated that EU-wide compliance with the EU ETS could be achieved for a carbon price of £40 per tonne by 2020. In a first instance, the same cut-off price of £40 per tonne was then used for emission reduction options outside the EU ETS (in the non-traded sector). However, in many cases more expensive measures were ultimately also included based on their 'dynamic efficiency' – that is, their long-term potential for deep emission cuts later on – or to start driving down the costs of promising technologies.

A distinction was made between the theoretically feasible potential and the realistically achievable potential, which takes into account barriers in the uptake of measures. The realistic potential reflects a judgement on the prevailing policy framework, how it might be strengthened and the incentives it gives to take up theoretically feasible abatement options. In this respect, the CCC distinguished between three policy scenarios (CCC, 2008):

- The *current ambition scenario* includes measures which cost less than the £40 per tonne cut-off, or which are covered by existing policies, but is cautious about their realistically achievable potential. The scenario includes significant progress towards low-carbon electricity generation, and some progress on improving fuel efficiency in new cars.
- The *extended ambition scenario* includes 'more ambitious but still reasonable assumptions' about the realistic reduction potential of existing policies, plus a number of measures which would cost more than £40 per tonne, but which are 'important stepping stones on the path to 2050'. The scenario is 'broadly in line' with policies to which the government or the EU are committed in principle, but which have yet to be implemented.
- The *stretch ambition scenario* adds further abatement options for which there is no policy commitment at the moment, for example 'more radical new technology deployment and more significant lifestyle adjustments'.

The conclusion of this analysis is that the 'extended ambition' scenario would be sufficient for the UK to meet the interim budget target. For the intended target, 'extended ambition' would have to be combined with an increased reliance on carbon offsets or additional measures envisaged under the 'stretch ambition scenario'. However, the existing policy framework will have to be strengthened to reach 'extended ambition' level or more.

The CCC looked in detail at the wider social and economic implications of the proposed budgets – on competitiveness, energy security, fuel poverty, the fiscal balance and for the devolved administrations. It found that they were on the whole manageable, although complementary measures may be needed to mitigate some of them, for example in the case of fuel poverty and the competitiveness of selected sectors. Overall, the CCC concluded that the UK could meet the proposed carbon budgets at a cost of less than 1 per cent of GDP.

4. The road ahead

The initial work of the CCC was about setting targets, both over the long term (2050) and more immediately for the first three carbon budgets (2008–2022). The CCC's recommendations on the long term were adopted straight away and are part of the Climate Change Act. In spring 2009 the government also adopted the CCC's 34 per cent interim target for 2008–2022. The government did not endorse the intended target of 42 per cent, but acknowledged the interim target will have to be revised once there is a new international agreement. The CCC will be asked for an updated recommendation once the details of the new agreement are known.

With advice on the fourth budget not due until 2010, the focus of the CCC is shifting to monitoring. Checking adherence to the carbon budgets is an important part of the remit of the CCC, which will assess progress in this respect in its annual reports to government. The immediate challenge for the 2009 annual report, due in October, will be to devise a framework of indicators that reveal, with sufficient lead time, whether the UK is on track in meeting its carbon budget obligations. Such lead indicators are likely to cover policy developments (e.g. changes to the renewable energy framework), implementation issues (e.g. uptake of new incentive schemes), investment (e.g. clean generation capacity under development), innovation (e.g. progress on CCS pilots) and technological change (e.g. the carbon efficiency of new cars). Particularly salient in the current economic environment will be the need to distinguish between structural, policy-induced change and temporary effects due, for example, to fluctuations in the business cycle.

The CCC will also seek to deepen its understanding of sectors and mitigation options that have not been fully covered in the first report. This includes, for example, the issue of agricultural emissions, technology options in the heating sector, demand-side measures in the transport sector and the impact of a large-scale shift to low-carbon technologies on the functioning of the electricity market. There is also the question of how to tackle airline emissions and bring international aviation and shipping into the carbon budgeting system. The role of aviation will be the subject of an aviation review carried out in 2009. Finally, the CCC will also start looking at adaptation with the creation of an adaptation sub-committee.

These questions are not new, and many of them will occupy analysts and policy makers for years to come as we seek to mitigate the risks of climate change. The work of the CCC, like the challenge of building a low-carbon economy, has only just started. But with the Climate Change Act the UK has put in place an institutional framework through which it can begin to tackle climate change.

Notes

1. However, concern about country allocation and accounting issues led the CCC not to recommend the inclusion of international aviation and shipping in the 2008–2022 budgets.
2. See www.cgd.ucar.edu/cas/wigley/magicc.

References

AEA, 2008. *MARKAL-MED Model Runs for Long-term Carbon Reduction Targets in the UK, Phase I and II*. Final Report to the Committee on Climate Change. www.theccc.org.uk/reports/building-a-low-carbon-economy/supporting-research.

Barker, T., Bashmakov, I., Alharthi, A., Amann, M., Cifuentes, L., Drexhage, J., Duan, M., Edenhofer, O., Flannery, B., Grubb, M., Hoogwijk, M., Ibitoye, F. I., Jepma, C. J., Pizer, W. A. and Yamaji, K., 2007. Mitigation from a cross-sectoral perspective. *Climate Change 2007: Mitigation of Climate Change*. Contribution of Working Group III to the Fourth Assessment Report of the Intergovernmental Panel on Climate Change (IPPC). Cambridge University Press, Cambridge, UK.

CCC (Committee on Climate Change), 2008. *Building a Low Carbon Economy: The UK's Contribution to Tackling Climate Change*. The First Report of the Committee on Climate Change, December. TSO, London. www.theccc.org.uk/reports/building-a-low-carbon-economy.

Dietz, S., 2008. *A Long-Run Target for Climate Policy: The Stern Review and its Critics*. Background Report for the Committee on Climate Change. Grantham Research Institute, London School of Economics, London. www.theccc.org.uk/reports/building-a-low-carbon-economy/supporting-research.

DTI, 2003. *Our Energy Future: Creating a Low Carbon Economy*. Energy White Paper, Department of Trade and Industry, February. TSO, London.

Meinshausen, M., Hare, B., Wigley, T. M. M., Van Vuuren, D., Den Elzen, M. G. J. and Swart, R., 2006. Multi-gas emissions pathways to meet climate targets. *Climatic Change*, 75(1). 151–194.

RCEP, 2000. *Energy – the Changing Climate*. Royal Commission on Environmental Pollution 22nd Report, June. www.rcep.org.uk/energy.htm.

Smith, J. B., Schellnhuber, H. J., Qader Mirza, M., Fankhauser, S., Leemans, R., Lin, E., Ogallo, L., Pittock, B., Richels, R., Rosenzweig, C., Safriel, U., Tol, R. S. J., Weyant, J. and Yohe, G., 2001. Lines of evidence for vulnerability of climate change: a synthesis. *Climate Change: Impacts, Adaptation and Vulnerability*. Contribution of Working Group II to the Third Assessment Report of the IPCC. Cambridge University Press, Cambridge, UK.

Smith, J. B., Schneider, S. H., Oppenheimer, M., Yohe, G. W., Hare, W., Mastrandrea, M. D., Patwardhan, A., Burton, I., Corfee-Morlot, J., Magadza, C. H. D., Füssel, H. M., Pittock, A. B., Rahman, A., Suarez, A. and van Ypersele, J. P., 2009. Assessing dangerous climate change through an update of the Intergovernmental Panel on Climate Change (IPCC) 'reasons for concern'. *Proceedings of the National Academy of Science USA*, 106(11). 4133–4137.

Solomon, S., Qin, D., Manning, M., Chen, Z., Marquis, M., Averyt, K. B., Tignor, M. and Miller, H. L. (eds), 2007. *Climate Change 2007: The Physical Science Basis*. Contribution of Working Group I to the Fourth Assessment Report of the Intergovernmental

Panel on Climate Change (IPCC). Cambridge University Press, Cambridge, UK.

Stern, N., 2008. *Key Elements of a Global Deal on Climate Change.* Grantham Research Institute, London School of Economics, London. www.lse.ac.uk/grantham.

Sura, K. and Golborne, N., 2008. Integrated assessment modelling. Technical appendix for Chapter 2. *Building a Low Carbon Economy: The UK's Contribution to Tackling Climate Change:* The First Report of the Committee on Climate Change, December. TSO, London. www.theccc.org.uk/reports/building-a-low-carbon-economy/supporting-research.

Watkiss, P., Blyth, W., Dietz, S., Downing, T., Hunt, A. and Fletcher, K., 2008. *Review of the Methodological Approaches Available to Set UK Carbon Budgets.* Report to the Shadow Committee on Climate Change, April. www.theccc.org.uk/reports/building-a-low-carbon-economy/supporting-research.

ENVIRONMENTAL
HAZARDS
Human and Policy Dimensions

research article

Managing natural disaster risks in a changing climate

W. J. W. BOTZEN[1],* AND J. C. J. M. VAN DEN BERGH[2]

[1]Institute for Environmental Studies, Vrije Universiteit, Amsterdam, The Netherlands
[2]ICREA, Barcelona, Spain; Institute of Environmental Science and Technology & Department of Economics and Economic History, Universitat Autònoma de Barcelona, Spain; Faculty of Economics and Business Administration & Institute for Environmental Studies, Vrije Universiteit, Amsterdam, The Netherlands

Natural disasters have increased in frequency and severity during the last few decades, causing considerable economic damage and loss of life. A combination of climate and socio-economic change is likely to augment disaster loss trends in the future, creating the need for more sophisticated disaster risk management. A resilient risk management strategy for uncertain low-probability, high-impact risks comprises a package of measures focused on disaster risk prevention, damage mitigation and arrangements for efficient risk sharing. Possible implications of climate change on future risks and risk management policies are outlined. It is argued that financial arrangements such as insurance can play an important role in an adaptation strategy aimed at limiting and ameliorating socio-economic impacts of natural disasters.

Keywords: adaptation; bounded rationality; catastrophe modelling; climate change; insurance; natural disasters; risk perception

1. Introduction

Recent extreme weather events have demonstrated the vulnerability of various countries to natural disasters (Munich Re, 2009). Economic losses caused by such disasters can be of such magnitude that individuals and businesses may be unable to carry them and could risk bankruptcy unless they are financially compensated. In the face of a projected rise in the frequency and severity of natural disasters due to socio-economic developments and climate change the question arises of how to design policies that limit exposure to and ameliorate impacts of natural disasters. The role of financial arrangements for natural disaster risk is important in this respect, since an often-raised question is who should pay for the elevated risks faced (Kunreuther et al., 2008). Apart from simply compensating for damage, financial arrangements such as insurance may contribute to the adaptation

of societies to increasing risk and enhance economic resilience to disasters (Mills and Lecompte, 2006; Botzen and van den Bergh, 2008). This is not an easy task for the insurance sector, given the problems with insuring low-probability, high-consequence (correlated) disaster risk. As an example, in the USA several major insurance companies retreated from some hazard-prone areas, such as State Farm in Florida, where hurricane risks are very high, as they were incapable of limiting exposure to rising risk (von Ungern-Sternberg, 2009).[1]

During the last few decades a considerable increase in the frequency and economic damage of natural disasters occurred worldwide (Kunreuther and Michel-Kerjan, 2007). Figure 1 shows an upward trend in overall and insured losses caused by great natural disasters since 1950. Natural disasters, such as major storms, floods and earthquakes, have devastating consequences for societies around the globe with

■ *Corresponding author. *E-mail:* **wouter.botzen@ivm.vu.nl**

ENVIRONMENTAL HAZARDS **8 (2009) 209–225**

doi:10.3763/ehaz.2009.0023 © 2009 Earthscan ISSN: 1747-7891 (print), 1878-0059 (online) www.earthscanjournals.com

earthscan

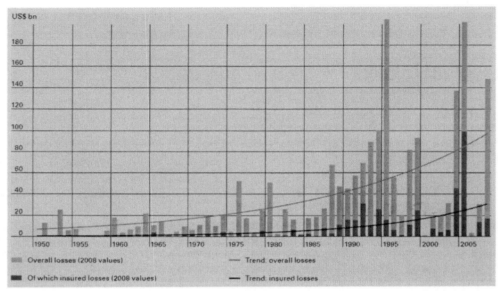

FIGURE 1 Overall and insured losses caused by great natural disasters between 1950 and 2008 (2008 values)

Source: Munich Re (2009).

especially large impacts on developing countries, while effects on insurers are concentrated in developed countries (Freeman et al., 2003). In particular, natural disasters may cause many deaths with a single event, resulting in the spread of diseases in affected areas, and have major adverse economic consequences caused by damage to property, both direct and indirect, such as business interruption and productivity losses. Some examples of major events in the last decade indicate the diversity of threats posed by nature and their global character. Major events in Europe were the 2002 floods in Central Europe, the 2003 heatwave that caused 35,000 deaths, and river floods in the UK in 2007. The tsunami in Asia in 2004 was a large catastrophe causing more than 283,000 deaths while a major earthquake in China caused at least 70,000 deaths in 2008 (Lay et al., 2005; Munich Re, 2009). The USA was hit by a series of destructive hurricanes in 2005 – hurricanes Katrina, Rita and Wilma killed over 1,500 people and resulted in USD180 billion of compensation payments – followed by hurricane Ike in 2008 (Kunreuther et al., 2008). Damaging wildfires occurred in Greece in 2008; major forest fires in Australia in

2009 killed over 200 people and damaged large pieces of land with devastating effects on wildlife.

The sharp increase in tempo and severity of the recent disasters made some leading academics suggest that we have entered a new era of natural catastrophes (Kunreuther et al., 2008). Because of their disruptive impacts[2] natural catastrophes are often well publicized in the media and are an important issue for governments, international organizations, such as the World Bank and the United Nations, and the broader research community. A question that often arises is how to design effective policies that limit the rise in natural disaster losses and reduce their impact on human societies. This paper provides some insights into this subject from an economics perspective and indicates the role financial arrangements can play in limiting exposure to natural disasters. The insurance sector, which is the world's largest industry in terms of revenues, could be a major partner in promoting climate change adaptation (Mills, 2007). In this respect climate change does not only pose a threat to insurers but also entails the development of new business opportunities (Mills, 2007; Botzen et al., 2009a).

The remainder of this paper is structured as follows: Section 2 outlines the influence of socio-economic developments and climate change on natural disaster risk; Section 3 discusses expert assessment of risk and households' perceptions and behavioural responses to risk; Section 4 provides some strategies of managing extreme weather risk; and Section 5 examines the role financial arrangements can play in natural disaster risk management.

2. Future natural disaster risk under climate and socio-economic change

2.1. Impact of socio-economic developments on natural catastrophe damage

Human-induced developments are a major determinant of the occurrence and consequences of natural disasters. Natural hazards such as storms, flash floods, heat waves and storm surges are natural phenomena. However, the damage caused by them is to a great extent influenced by human activities. A natural disaster is usually defined as the impact of a natural event on human societies, for example, in terms of loss of lives or economic costs (Bočkarjova, 2007). A certain threshold of economic damage or loss of life generally needs to be exceeded before an extreme weather event is defined as a natural disaster. Important in this respect are also the abilities of societies to prepare for and manage the economic disruption caused by the disaster, which depend on the countries' level of economic development (Rose, 2003). A major part of the increased damage due to natural disasters around the globe can be explained by socio-economic developments such as an increased population and concentration of wealth in areas that are vulnerable to natural hazards (Changnon, 2003; Muir-Wood et al., 2006; Crompton and McAneney, 2008; Miller et al., 2008). For example, the large rise in hurricane damage in the USA that has been observed in the last decades is mainly due to increased human settlements at coastal locations where hurricanes often make landfall, such as Florida (Pielke et al., 2008; Schmidt et al., 2009). In the future, urbanization in hazard-prone areas such as coastal agglomerations is projected to continue, which enhances vulnerability to weather extremes, posing challenges for the management of natural disaster risk (Bouwer et al., 2007).

2.2. Climate change and the frequency and severity of natural disasters

In addition to socio-economic developments, climate change may increase the intensity and severity of weather extremes and contribute to an increasing loss burden of natural disasters in the future (Mills, 2005; IPCC, 2007; Botzen et al., 2009a). Anthropogenic climate change is caused by the emissions of carbon dioxide and other greenhouse gases such as methane which have accumulated in the earth's atmosphere since the industrial revolution (mainly since the late 19th century), predominantly due to the burning of fossil fuels, deforestation and other land use changes. These rising levels of greenhouse gases result in increases in surface air temperature, because the greenhouse gases in the atmosphere trap heat (e.g. Pierrehumbert, 2004). The Intergovernmental Panel on Climate Change (IPCC) projects a rise in global average surface temperatures between 1.1 and 2.9°C in 2100 for a low-emission scenario and between 2.4 and 6.4°C in 2100 under a high-emission scenario (IPCC, 2007). Several positive feedback mechanisms of climate change may increase greenhouse gas concentrations in addition to human-induced emissions and, therefore, result in more warming than anticipated by climate models (Stern, 2007). Examples are releases of methane due to melting of permafrost and a reduced uptake of carbon as a result of the weakening of natural carbons sinks, such as the Amazon forest[3] (Heimann and Reichstein, 2008; Kennedy et al., 2008).

Climate change is likely to result in an intensified water cycle, which implies that existing regional patterns of scarcity and abundance of water are amplified, increasing the risk of droughts and floods. In particular, rainfall and floods are likely to increase in high latitude regions, while southern arid regions are expected to have considerable reductions in rainfall in both hemispheres. In other parts of the world, warmer air and oceans could cause more intense storms, such as hurricanes and typhoons. In addition, climate change is expected to cause a rise in the mean sea level due to expansion of warmer oceans and melting of glaciers and ice caps. The IPCC (2007) projects a global rise in sea levels of 0.2–0.6 m by 2100. An irreversible melting of Greenland ice[4] or a collapse of the West-Antarctic Ice Sheet (which has a low probability of occurring) could cause a substantial rise in sea level of about 5–12 m globally, although this is very uncertain and could only occur in the course of several centuries (Rapley, 2006; Wood et al., 2006). Sea level rise will inundate many unprotected low-lying areas, and may increase the likelihood of flooding due to storm surges, which could have considerable consequences for small island states and countries with extensively populated deltas and coastal areas, such as the Netherlands, Vietnam and Bangladesh.

The IPCC (2007) states that global temperatures have increased by approximately 0.76°C since 1900 while sea levels rose by about 20 cm. There is also evidence that some of these expected effects of climate change on extreme weather have already materialized. The IPCC (2007) indicates that it is likely that both heatwaves and heavy precipitation events increased in frequency during the late 20th century over most areas and that it is more likely than not that humans contributed to the observed trend. Moreover, an increased incidence of extreme high sea levels has been observed over this time period and it is more likely than not that humans also contributed to this trend. According to the IPCC (2007) there has been evidence of an increase in the average intensity of tropical cyclones such as hurricanes and typhoons in the North Atlantic and some other regions since the 1970s and that it is more likely than not that the trend has been influenced by anthropogenic climate change. A recent study

by Elsner et al. (2008) shows that upward trends for wind speeds of strong hurricanes can be observed in each relevant ocean basin.

There is, however, still debate in the scientific community about whether the upswing in hurricane activity is caused by anthropogenic climate change, meaning that it is likely to persist in the future, or natural climate variability related to the Atlantic Multidecadal Oscillation (Kerr, 2006). Some research suggests that global warming has already resulted in an increased intensity or frequency of hurricanes, and that this may have been caused by higher sea surface temperatures (e.g. Emanuel, 2005; Webster et al., 2005; Hoyos et al., 2006). Saunders and Lea (2008) estimate the contribution of sea surface temperature on hurricane frequency and activity for the USA and conclude that a 0.5°C increase in sea temperature is associated with a 40 per cent increase in hurricane frequency and activity. However, it has been argued that current observation databases are insufficiently reliable to analyse trends of hurricane activity due to subjective measurement and variable procedures over time. Also, time periods used may be too short to draw definite conclusions about climate change (Landsea et al., 2006; Michaels, 2006). This is likely to remain an active and very relevant area of research in the near future, given the high insured and economic costs hurricanes may cause (e.g. Höppe and Pielke, 2006).

Climate change may be seen as an externality of economic activities, since individuals and businesses that pollute the atmosphere with greenhouse gas emissions, for example, through electricity generation, driving, flying and destruction of forests, do not pay for the costs of climate change that are caused by increased atmospheric greenhouse concentrations. Internalizing these costs for economic agents around the globe via taxes, regulation or emissions trading systems is complicated by the public good and global nature of the atmosphere and resulting problems with free-riding behaviour. For these reasons, it is difficult to reach the stringent international agreement on greenhouse gas emissions that is required for stabilizing or reducing atmospheric concentrations of greenhouse gases. Future greenhouse gas emissions may rise rapidly due to the fast industrialization of Asian economies with increasing demands for energy (Botzen et al., 2008). Nevertheless, even in the unlikely case that emissions could be reduced to zero, warming would continue for several decades because of the lag in response time of the climate system caused, among others, by the past emissions that persist in the atmosphere for a very long time. This highlights the necessity of examining the effects of climate change on extreme weather events and resultant damage and designing adequate adaptation policies to manage potential changes in these risks (Pielke et al., 2007).

3. Assessing natural catastrophe risk

3.1. Expert modelling of natural disaster risk

Assessments of future risk are inherently difficult because of the uncertainties associated with the impacts of climate change and socio-economic development on future natural disaster risk (IPCC, 2007). Considerable uncertainty and ambiguity is associated with both the frequency of a disaster occurring and the damage that it will cause. Constructing different scenarios of climate and socio-economic change and estimating their influence on risk may be a useful first step in assessing future risk. Statistical models can be used to assess how frequencies and severities of natural disaster or disaster damage relate to variability in climate (e.g. Saunders and Lea, 2008; Schmidt et al., 2009). Extrapolations of such historical relations under changes in climate conditions may then provide insights into future risks (e.g. Botzen et al., 2009b). Moreover, catastrophe models are commonly used to assess exposure to natural disaster risk (Grossi and Kunreuther, 2005). Such computer-based models estimate the loss potential of catastrophes by overlaying the properties at risk and the potential sources of natural hazards in a specific geographical area with the use of Geographic Information Systems (GIS).

FIGURE 2 Main components of catastrophe models
Source: Adapted from Grossi and Kunreuther (2005)

Figure 2 shows a schematic overview of the main components of catastrophe models (Grossi and Kunreuther, 2005). The natural hazard module of a model characterizes the physical characteristics of the hazard, such as the location of a flood, flood depth and flow velocities of water, wind speeds, and frequency of occurrence of the hazard. The portfolio of properties at risk component of the model can include various characteristics of assets, such as the location, age and type of buildings or land use. The vulnerability component of the model quantifies the impact of the natural hazard on the properties at risk, which may be done by the use of damage curves that describe the relation of physical parameters, e.g. flood depth, with damage to the inventory, such as flood damage to buildings (e.g. Merz et al., 2004). The resulting damage to the portfolio of properties is computed based on these vulnerability measures and may consist of direct losses, indirect losses or both. The output of such models may be represented as exceedance probability curves that indicate the probability of a certain loss being surpassed or geographical maps that show levels of risk (Bouwer et al., 2009; de Moel et al., 2009). Examples of users of catastrophe models are insurers who use them to assess their financial exposure to natural hazards and governments that are interested in evaluating the geographical exposure to risks or the effectiveness of protection measures, such as dikes or building codes.

Over time, catastrophe models need to be updated due to socio-economic developments and climate change. In case climate change increases the frequency or severity of extreme weather, the 'natural hazard' component of the model needs to be adjusted to reflect increased risks. Socio-economic developments, such as increased urbanization in hazard-prone areas, may require changes in the 'portfolio of properties at risk' component over time.

As an illustration, Aerts et al. (2008a) have estimated the independent influence of climate change and socio-economic developments on flood risk, defined as *probability $_*$ damage*, in the Netherlands until the year 2100. Two extremes were studied in order to gain insights into the effect of urban growth on the one hand and climate change on the other.[5] Effects of climate change were modelled using three sea level rise scenarios of 60, 85 and 150 cm per 100 years, which influence the flood probability ('natural hazard' component in Figure 2). Furthermore, changes in urban development were assessed using two scenarios, namely low economic growth (RC) and high growth (GE) and corresponding changes in the 'portfolio of properties at risk' module of Figure 2 were based on a land use model of the Netherlands (Janssen et al., 2006). The results shown in Figure 3 indicate that a moderate rise in sea level of 60 cm results in a similar increase in potential damage as a high economic growth scenario. Climate change effects only dominate for very high increases in sea level. These results indicate the importance of directing adaptation policies to limit both a possible rise in probabilities and damage caused by natural disasters (see Section 4).

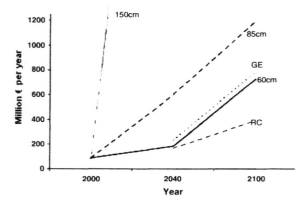

FIGURE 3 Assessment of future flood risk in the Netherlands under a range of climate change and socio-economic scenarios

Source: Aerts et al. (2008a)

3.2. Households' assessments of risk and behaviour

3.2.1. Individual risk perception

In evaluating hazards people commonly rely on intuitive risk judgements, known as risk perceptions, which often differ considerably from expert assessments (Slovic, 1987; 2000). The understanding of risk perception of individuals is very important in designing adaptation policies. Household risk judgements can determine the perceived legitimacy as well as compliance with land-use planning and other adaptation policies (Peacock et al., 2005). Moreover, individual perceptions of hazards are important factors behind decision making under risk with respect to insurance purchases and the undertaking of self-protective measures (Burn, 1999; Flynn et al., 1999; Botzen et al., 2009c).

Individuals often use simple rules when they assess risks, which may be described as heuristics (Kahneman et al., 1982). Individuals may use the 'availability heuristic' in judging natural hazard risk, which implies that they judge an event as risky if it is easy to imagine or recall. For example, individuals who have experienced a disaster may find it easier to imagine that the disaster will happen again in the future and therefore indicate a higher perceived risk than individuals without this experience. Individuals often rely on affective feelings when they judge the level of risks, which may deviate from pure logical and analytical reasoning (Loewenstein et al., 2001; Slovic et al., 2004). Individuals may have a higher risk perception if natural hazards are associated with negative feelings, which may have been caused or reinforced by experiences with damage caused by natural hazards or evacuation because of disaster (Finucane et al., 2000; Keller et al., 2006). Often natural disasters have very low frequencies of occurrence so that individuals may have a very low risk perception or even neglect the risk altogether (Botzen et al., 2009d). Governments can undertake information campaigns if individual risk perceptions deviate considerably from expert risk judgements.

3.2.2. Individual behaviour under risk

Economists commonly use the expected utility framework in analysing individual decision making under risk, such as insurance purchases. However, in many cases this framework fails to adequately describe behaviour in practice, especially in the case of low-probability, high-impact risks such as natural disasters (e.g. Mason et al., 2005). A reason for this is that individuals often deviate from rational behavioural principles when they make decisions under risk (Kahneman, 2003). In particular, a common observation is that individuals either overestimate or neglect low-probability risk (Tversky and Kahneman, 1992). This processing of risk poses some difficulties when applying the traditional expected utility framework of individual decision making under risk (von Neumann and Morgenstern, 1947), which assumes that individuals correctly assess the likelihoods of adverse events and that individuals process probabilities linearly. The descriptive failure of expected utility theory in explaining individual behaviour under risk is well documented (Camerer, 1998). Alternative theories that allow for the modelling of individual attitudes toward probabilities or 'probability weighting' may be more suitable to model individual behaviour. Important examples are prospect theory and rank-dependent utility theory (Kahneman and Tversky, 1979; Quiggin, 1982; Schmeidler, 1989; Tversky and Kahneman, 1992). Allowing for 'bounded rationality' or limitations in individuals' perceptive and cognitive capabilities is fundamental in correctly anticipating individual responses to risky events, such as demand for insurance coverage against natural disasters (Botzen and van den Bergh, 2009a).

4. Managing natural hazards risks

4.1. Economic resilience to natural disasters

A potentially important concept in managing natural disaster risk is the notion of resilience, even though its broad meaning has obstructed its use in risk management (Klein et al., 2003). As Bočkarjova (2007) and Rose (2007) discuss, resilience has been defined differently in various disciplines, such as ecology (from where the concept originates), engineering and economics, as well as between various authors. Resilience has two main interpretations, namely the time necessary for a disturbed system to return to its original state (Pimm, 1984) and the amount of disturbance a system can absorb before moving to another state (Holling, 1973; 1986). Rose (2004b), who defines resilience from an economics perspective, relates resilience to the time needed for recovery in the aftermath of a disaster in the sense that a higher level of resilience allows the economy to recover faster at lower costs. Moreover, Rose (2004a; 2006) regards resilience as a post-disaster characteristic that comprises the inherent and adaptive responses to disasters that result in the avoidance of potential losses. In his definition, resilience encompasses the ability of societies to limit or prevent losses during and after a disaster, and emphasizes ingenuity and resourcefulness applied.

In the context of climate change Timmerman (1981) defines resilience as the capacity to absorb and recover from the occurrence of a hazardous event. Resilience is related to adaptation, which comprises adjustments ex ante of the occurrence of a disaster aimed at creating conditions within the human system that enhance this system's resistance to disasters and its capacity to respond to, and cushion impacts of, a disaster (Handmer and Dovers, 1996; Bočkarjova, 2007). Bočkarjova (2007) adds to the definition of resilience the ability of the human-induced system to exhibit learning so as to improve its protective mechanisms (adaptation) in the face of disasters. Resilience may be spatially dependent and differ between regions within the same country. For example, Porfiriev (2009) argues that megacities may have a higher resilience capacity than small towns, because the latter often lack economic resources to ameliorate impacts of a disaster. Climate change increases the need for resilience since it may lead to more disturbances of the human system due to an increased frequency and severity of weather extremes. Improving resilience (according to the aforementioned definitions) and adaptive capacity may thus be seen as a desirable policy instrument to manage natural disaster risks (Tobin, 1999).

4.2. Risk management strategies

4.2.1. Hazard prevention to reduce the probability of suffering damage and expected costs of damage

Preventing the hazard from occurring and reducing the probability or expected costs of suffering damage is an effective strategy for limiting risk of certain natural hazards, such as flooding, while it may be more difficult for others, such as storms. Examples of strategies that limit the probability of suffering damage are the creation of dams for flood control, dikes, storm surge barriers and relocation of property out of hazard-prone areas. Investments in hazard prevention are usually undertaken by governments because of the public good characteristics of protection of infrastructure. There seems to be considerable scope to improve cost-effective prevention or damage mitigation strategies worldwide. It has been suggested that worldwide investments of USD40 billion in disaster preparedness, prevention and mitigation would have reduced global economic losses by USD280 billion during the 1990s (IFRC, 2001).

Public support for large investments in protection infrastructure often only arises after a disaster has occurred. For example, strategies to prevent flood damage are well developed in countries around the North Sea and in Japan, where flooding claimed many lives until the middle of the 20th century. After a catastrophic flood in 1953 the Dutch built their famous Deltaworks; a series of dams, sluices, dikes and storm surge barriers constructed between 1958 and 1997 in the south-west of the Netherlands (Aerts and Botzen, 2009). This flood protection infrastructure was successful in ensuring high safety standards that in some areas protect against

storm surges with a recurrence interval of 1 in 10,000 years. Cost–benefit analysis may guide the determination of safety standards and protection investments, as has been done in the Netherlands (van Dantzig, 1956; Jonkman et al., 2004). A drawback of hazard prevention with engineering infrastructure is that it may be perceived by households and companies that the risk is eliminated instead of reduced, which can encourage economic development in hazardous areas (Vis et al., 2003).

Once in place, a continuous updating of protection infrastructure is needed, notably in areas that are impacted by a rapid increase in the frequency of hazards due to climate change or by an increase in potential damage that may be caused by socio-economic developments in the protected areas. A proactive or anticipatory approach that reduces vulnerability before climate change results in adverse impacts, such as floods, may be desirable (Klein et al., 2003). The success of measures limiting risk will depend on the magnitude and rate of change of the climate; large changes that occur rapidly may be difficult to accommodate. Large regional variations exist in climate change impacts indicating that a variety of strategies needs to be implemented in different areas that may be affected by higher flood, drought or storm risks (IPCC, 2007).

Current prevention measures may be inadequate to deal with climate change. For example, at this moment, the storm surge barriers of the Deltaworks in the Netherlands are insufficiently prepared for (further) rises in sea level and are likely to require adjustments in the future. A cost–benefit analysis performed by Aerts and Botzen (2009) of the 'Haringvliet' barrier that is part of the Deltaworks indicates that adapting the barrier to climate change instead of replacing it completely is a good investment. Unfortunately, adjusting the construction of some barriers to sea level rise is not possible. In designing hazard prevention or damage mitigation measures it is, therefore, advisable to consider flexible infrastructure that allows for adjustments to climate change, especially given the considerable uncertainty that is associated with sea level rise projections (IPCC, 2007).

4.2.2. Mitigation of damage at the household level

The undertaking of measures that mitigate damage at the household level may be an effective strategy to reduce risks. Such mitigation measures could prevent or limit damage once a natural hazard takes place. Examples are anchoring roofs to withstand strong winds, creating flexible buildings that do not collapse during earthquakes, or investing in water barriers or 'flood proofing' of houses. Several studies suggest that cost savings of mitigation can be considerable.

Kunreuther et al. (2008) model hurricane damage in New York, Texas, South Carolina and Florida in situations with and without mitigation according to recent building code standards. The results for a 100-year hurricane indicate that mitigation could reduce potential losses by 61 per cent in Florida, 44 per cent in South Carolina, 39 per cent in New York and 34 per cent in Texas. Savings in Florida alone due to mitigation would result in USD51 billion for a 100-year and USD83 billion for a 500-year event. Experience of flooding in Europe also indicates that households avoided considerable flood damage due to the implementation of damage mitigation measures. The damage incurred by the 2002 flood in the river Elbe in Germany could be limited by changing the buildings' design and mode of use. This implies that cellars and storeys exposed to flooding are not used intensively, waterproof construction materials are used and easily movable furniture is placed on the lower floors (Kreibich et al., 2005; Thieken et al., 2005; 2006). In particular, use of buildings and interior fitting adapted to flooding reduced damage to buildings by 46 and 53 per cent, and damage to contents by 48 and 53 per cent, respectively (Kreibich et al., 2005).

Given the efficiency of mitigation in managing natural disaster risk, further research should focus on identifying cost-effective mitigation measures and how individuals can be stimulated to invest in mitigation, which is likely to depend, among other things, on risk perception. Insurance arrangements could be useful in achieving the latter, as will be elaborated upon in Section 5.

4.2.3. Damage compensation

Governments are often under considerable pressure to compensate households and businesses financially after natural disasters (e.g. Downton and Pielke, 2001). Compensation for such damage can facilitate the process of economic recovery after a catastrophe. It can also accelerate the rebuilding of damaged property and prevent bankruptcy of individual households and firms, thereby adding to continuity of business operations and stimulating rebuilding of the capital stock. An efficient financial arrangement for compensation of disaster damage may therefore contribute to economic resilience (Pelling, 2003; Rose, 2007).

However, compensation for flood damage may also provide incentives to take risk instead of reducing it, if a compensation arrangement is inadequately designed. Incentives to settle in safe areas instead of risk-prone areas are minimal in cases where governments compensate damage unconditionally against the risk taken by households who settle in risky areas. In the same venue of a moral hazard effect, incentives for households to limit losses and invest in mitigation measures are minimal in cases where governments generously compensate the damage caused by natural disasters (e.g. Priest, 1996). Moreover, uncertainty associated with ad hoc compensation schemes that exist in some countries, such as the Netherlands, may be undesirable from the perspective of welfare of risk-averse individuals (Botzen and van den Bergh, 2008). Well-designed insurance arrangements for compensating natural disaster losses may overcome such complications (see Section 5).

4.2.4. Diversification of risk management strategies

The combination of climate and socio-economic change that will influence future natural disaster losses results in inherently uncertain changes in risks. A characteristic of a resilient system is that it is diverse, meaning that a number of functionally different components protect the system from various threats in a diversified portfolio (Godschalk, 2003). Hence, a resilient natural hazard risk management strategy necessarily involves a package of actions (de Bruijn et al., 2007). De Bruijn and Klijn (2001) and Vis et al. (2003) argue that resilient flood risk management aims at both lowering the probability of the hazard occurring and reducing its possible impact, i.e. damage. The latter authors suggest that implementing strategies that aim at lowering flood damage in the Netherlands via compartments and green rivers that allow for water storage during peak discharges are a useful and resilient strategy for long-term flood risk management. The objective for policy makers is to find an optimal portfolio of protection measures that prevent and limit damage during and after events. Aerts et al. (2008b) examine this for investments in flood control in the Netherlands using a portfolio framework that aims for the highest mean and lowest variance in return (avoided damage). Combining investments in dikes to reduce the probability of inundation with investments in flood proofing provides for reduction in risk of extremely large damage compared with investments in dikes alone.

5. Role of insurance in adaptation to natural disasters

5.1. Climate change impact on the insurance sector

The insurance sector covers a considerable part of weather-related risk, especially in developed countries (Hoff et al., 2005).[6] Future insurance claims may increase considerably if climate change projections and socio-economic developments result in an increased frequency and magnitude of natural disaster damage (Dlugolecki, 2000; 2008; Vellinga et al., 2001; Mills, 2005). From an insurer's perspective the time pattern of

losses due to socio-economic developments is likely to cause fewer problems than the effects of climate change on disaster damage. The reason is that a rise in population and wealth which increases the monetary value insured automatically results in a similar rise in premium revenues, thereby balancing expected insurance payouts and premium revenues.

In contrast, if climate change increases risks then premium income will lag behind payouts of claims, unless premiums are adjusted (Mills et al., 2002). The best strategy for insurers would be to incorporate expected changes in probabilities of weather extremes in assessing exposure to, and pricing and management of, risk (Botzen et al., 2009a). In practice, this may be difficult since the low-probability nature of extreme weather events complicates the assessment of climate change impacts on loss trends. Moreover, considerable uncertainty is associated with projected effects of climate change on natural disasters and resulting damage (IPCC, 2007). After the experience of the devastating hurricane season in 2005 in the USA the question arose whether climate change caused an increase in hurricane activity and frequency, requiring insurance premium adjustments, or whether average hurricane frequencies had not changed and the 2005 hurricane season reflected natural climate variability (see Section 2). One of the main catastrophe modelling firms, Risk Management Solutions (RMS), projected an increase in hurricane frequency and severity and advised increased premiums. Insurance regulators resisted this adjustment in premiums, arguing that rates should be based only on historical losses and not reflect predictions (Kunreuther et al., 2008).

In general, one should not constrain the ability of insurers to adjust premiums according to changes in risk since this could impair the economic viability and solvency of insurers in the face of climate change. The flexible nature of the insurance business with short-term contracts and the ability to change premiums and coverage over time is a desirable characteristic to ensure resilience of the sector to climate change impacts (Vellinga et al., 2001).

Regional assessments of insurers' exposure to natural hazards and regional climate change projections of extreme weather risks can be useful information for premium setting and the risk management of insurance companies. The insurance sector could also play an important role in stimulating and promoting adaptation policies, which limit risks, as we will elaborate upon below. Indeed, climate change is not only a threat for insurers but presents new profitable business opportunities, such as offering insurance products for greenhouse gas mitigation technologies and projects (Mills, 2007).

5.2. Demand for financial coverage in a changing climate

Homeowners usually demand financial compensation for damage caused by natural hazards, which can be provided by government relief or insurance arrangements. Consumers' willingness to pay (WTP) for financial coverage via insurance schemes is expected to increase if climate change results in an increased frequency or severity of natural hazards (Botzen and van den Bergh, 2009a). If changes in households' WTP under climate change develop in line with changes in expected losses of the insurance, premium changes may have little impact on levels of insurance penetration. Quantitative modelling of insurance demand provides insights into effects of risk and premium changes on market shares of insurers (Botzen and van den Bergh, 2009b).

In modelling insurance demand under climate change it is important to account for bounded rationality and the commonly observed failure of expected utility theory in the context of low-probability, high-impact risk (see Section 3). In addition to changes in demand for existing insurance arrangements, climate change may also raise demand for new financial arrangements. Valuation techniques of consumers' preferences, such as surveys with contingent valuation and choice modelling methods (Mitchell and Carson, 1989), can be useful means to assess demand for new insurance products. For example, Akter

et al. (2009) estimated demand for crop insurance against flood damage in Bangladesh using the contingent valuation method. Their results indicate that crop insurance is (marginally) commercially viable in riverine flood plain areas, since expected WTP values exceed expected payouts of insurance. Such studies of insurance demand provide important information to policy makers and insurers about the feasibility of introducing new financial arrangements against natural hazard risks.

5.3. Role of insurers in managing natural disaster risk

It is useful to explore the role that insurance arrangements can play in managing natural disaster risk and promoting adaptation to possible increases in risk of extreme weather due to climate change (Botzen and van den Bergh, 2008). Insurers collect premiums from many individuals to be able to pay for damage caused by natural disasters that is very large for individual households and companies. In this way, insurance arrangements reduce individual loss exposures and thus spread risks. Primary insurers may further pool such natural disaster risk with other types of risk they insure and hedge risk by buying reinsurance coverage from reinsurance companies that spread risk on large geographical markets or hedge risk on capital markets using weather derivatives, such as catastrophe bonds, options and futures (Michel-Kerjan and Morlaye, 2008). This risk-spreading function of insurance may be welfare-enhancing for risk-averse individuals since it improves financial security (Botzen and van den Bergh, 2009a). Indeed, research on the effects of flood disasters on reported life satisfaction in 16 European countries indicates that decreased levels of life satisfaction usually observed after flood events are not present in regions with flood insurance (Luechinger and Raschky, 2009).

In addition to providing financial security, insurance arrangements may contribute to limiting damage caused by natural disaster by acting as a price signal for risk and promoting the undertaking of mitigation measures (Kunreuther, 1996; Botzen and van den Bergh, 2008). A necessary condition for this is that insurance premiums reflect the risk faced by the insured property (Kunreuther et al., 2008). Risk-based insurance premiums could act as a price signal for settling in an area and thus stimulate development in less risky areas and restrain development in hazard-prone areas, since premiums would be higher in the latter. Moreover, insurance can provide incentives to homeowners to invest in measures that mitigate damage. This is very relevant since practical experience shows that, although mitigation measures could be useful to manage risks, individuals rarely undertake them (Kunreuther, 2006a). Insurance can require the undertaking of mitigation in policy conditions or reward insured who invest in mitigation measures with premium discounts or increased levels of coverage (e.g. Kleindorfer and Kunreuther, 1999; Kunreuther and Pauly, 2006; Botzen et al., 2009c). Further research could explore whether such economic incentives are effective in encouraging investments that mitigate damage.

Several characteristics of natural disaster risk complicate insurance in (pure) private markets (Freeman and Kunreuther, 2003). The low-probability nature of natural hazard risk makes it difficult to assess the frequency of hazards and resulting damage and to determine adequate premiums. Catastrophe models may aid rate setting by insurers, but involve uncertainties, too. Moreover, natural hazards are correlated and impacts can be very large, so that insurees may face many losses when a disaster occurs that could be beyond the capacity of insurers to reimburse. For these reasons public–private partnerships in covering natural disaster risks could be explored in which governments cover part of the extreme tail of the loss distribution (Kunreuther, 2006b; Michel-Kerjan and de Marcellis-Warin, 2006; Botzen and van den Bergh, 2008). In designing such partnerships it is important that the aforementioned desirable characteristics of insurance in managing disaster risk and fostering adaptation are preserved.

6. Conclusions

The recent upswing in natural disaster occurrence and resulting damage illustrates the vulnerability of human societies to extreme weather events, such as storms, floods and droughts. Considerable research efforts have been devoted to examining whether trends in past losses have been influenced by climate change and concluded that socio-economic developments were the main cause behind the rapid increase in damage. Nevertheless, climate change projections indicate that in the future an increased frequency and severity of weather events may further increase losses, requiring innovative adaptation policies to manage risks. Regional projections of climate and socio-economic change and modelling of future changes in natural disaster risks are needed to steer adaptation and risk management strategies. An understanding of households' perceptions of risk is important in this respect as well. Perceptions may deviate from expert assessments and influence risk management of households, such as investments in precautionary measures or insurance purchases. A combination of investments in damage mitigation measures by households and prevention undertaken by the public sector is likely to result in well-diversified risk management strategies that enhance economic resilience to natural hazards.

The experience of the insurance sector in assessing, managing and spreading risks may be useful in fostering adaptation of modern societies to climate change. Well-designed financial compensation arrangements can speed up the recovery process after natural disasters have struck and can contribute to overall economic resilience. Moreover, insurance with risk-based premiums can provide economic incentives to limit damage by acting as a price signal of risks. Evidently, insuring climate change risks will not solve the adverse economic impacts of a higher frequency of natural disasters in the future, but it may ameliorate them. A main message of this article is that it is worthwhile exploring the complementary role that financial arrangements can play in designing comprehensive climate change adaptation policies that comprise risk prevention, reduction and efficient risk-sharing strategies.

Acknowledgements

We thank Laurens Bouwer and Boris Profiriev for helpful comments on this paper. This research project was carried out as part of the Dutch National Research Programme 'Climate Changes Spatial Planning' (www.klimaatvoorruimte.nl). The usual disclaimer applies.

Notes

1. The largest property insurer of Florida, State Farm, announced on 27 January 2009 that it will not renew its property insurances in the state, and halted all sales. This announcement followed the disapproval by regulators of a proposed premium increase by State Farm of 47 per cent to cover increased hurricane risks (www.statefarm.com).
2. Some authors argue that effects of catastrophes are minor in macroeconomic terms, even though natural catastrophes have considerable local impacts (Albala-Bertrand, 2006).
3. Deforestation may also increase the vulnerability to disasters caused by climate change, for example, because of soil erosion and landslides resulting from more frequent and severe rains and floods.
4. The surface mass balance of the Greenland Ice Sheet may turn negative at a global average warming larger than 1.9–4.6°C, which could result in its complete elimination over a very long time period (IPCC, 2007).
5. In this study it is assumed that no preventative measures will be undertaken to highlight the relative importance of socio-economic vs. climate change (Aerts et al., 2008a).
6. The insurance sector is here broadly defined as comprising both primary insurers and reinsurance companies. Reinsurance companies, such Munich Re and Swiss Re, are often the 'last resort' carriers of catastrophe risk. Potential effects of climate change are likely to be passed on from reinsurance companies to primary insurers in the form of higher reinsurance prices or reduced reinsurance coverage.

References

Aerts, J. C. J. H. and Botzen, W. J. W., 2009. The delta plan of the Netherlands: past and future perspectives on flood risk protection. *Against the Deluge: Storm Surge Barriers to Protect New York City*. Conference Proceedings, Polytechnic Institute of New York University, Brooklyn, NY.

Aerts, J. C. J. H., Sprong, T. and Bannink, B., 2008a. *Aandacht voor Veiligheid*. Vrije Universiteit Amsterdam, Amsterdam.

Aerts, J., Botzen, W. J. W., van der Veen, A., Krywkow, J. and Werners, S., 2008b. Dealing with uncertainty in flood management through diversification. *Ecology and Society*, 13(1). 41.

Akter, S., Brouwer, R., Choudhury, S. and Aziz, S., 2009. Is there a commercially viable market for crop insurance in rural Bangladesh? *Mitigation and Adaptation Strategies for Global Change*, 14(3). 215–229.

Albala-Bertrand, J. M., 2006. *The Unlikeliness of an Economic Catastrophe: Localization and Globalization*. Working Paper No. 576. Queen Mary College, University of London, London.

Bočkarjova, M., 2007. *Major Disasters in Modern Economies: An Input–Output Based Approach at Modelling Imbalances and Disproportions*. Doctoral dissertation, University of Twente, Enschede.

Botzen, W. J. W. and van den Bergh, J. C. J. M., 2008. Insurance against climate change and flooding in the Netherlands: present, future and comparison with other countries. *Risk Analysis*, 28(2). 413–426.

Botzen, W. J. W. and van den Bergh, J. C. J. M., 2009a. Bounded rationality, climate risks and insurance: is there a market for natural disasters? *Land Economics*, 85(2). 266–279.

Botzen, W. J. W. and van den Bergh, J. C. J. M., 2009b. Monetary valuation of insurance against climate change risk, submitted.

Botzen, W. J. W., Gowdy, J. M. and van den Bergh, J. C. J. M., 2008. Cumulative CO_2 emissions: shifting international responsibilities for climate debt. *Climate Policy*, 8. 569–576.

Botzen, W. J. W., van den Bergh, J. C. J. M. and Bouwer, L. M., 2009a. Climate change and increased risk for the insurance sector: a global perspective and an assessment for the Netherlands. *Natural Hazards*, forthcoming.

Botzen, W. J. W., Bouwer, L. M. and van den Bergh, J. C. J. M., 2009b. Climate change and hailstorm damage: empirical evidence and implications for agriculture and insurance, forthcoming.

Botzen, W. J. W., Aerts, J. C. J. H. and van den Bergh, J. C. J. M., 2009c. Willingness of homeowners to mitigate climate risk through insurance. *Ecological Economics*, 68(8–9). 2265–2277.

Botzen, W. J. W., Aerts, J. C. J. H. and van den Bergh, J. C. J. M., 2009d. Dependence of flood risk perceptions on socio-economic and objective risk factors. *Water Resources Research*, forthcoming.

Bouwer, L. M., Crompton, R. P., Faust, E., Höppe, P. and Pielke Jr., R.A., 2007. Confronting disaster losses. *Science*, 318(5851). 753.

Bouwer, L. M., Bubeck, P. and Aerts, J. C. J. H., 2009. *Future Flood Risk Estimates in a Dutch Polder Area*. Working manuscript. Institute for Environmental Studies, Vrije Universiteit, Amsterdam.

Burn, D. H., 1999. Perceptions of flood risk: a case study of the Red River flood of 1997. *Water Resources Research*, 35(11). 3451–3458.

Camerer, C., 1998. Bounded rationality in individual decision making. *Experimental Economics*, 1(2). 163–183.

Changnon, S. A., 2003. Shifting economic impacts from weather extremes in the United States: a result of societal changes, not global warming. *Natural Hazards*, 29(2). 273–290.

Crompton, R. P. and McAneney, K. J., 2008. Normalised Australian insured losses from meteorological hazards: 1967–2006. *Environmental Science & Policy*, 11(5). 371–378.

de Bruijn, K. M. and Klijn, F., 2001. Resilient flood risk management strategies. *Proceedings of the IAHR Congress 2001*, L. Guifen and L. Wenxue (eds). Tsinghua University Press, Beijing.

de Bruijn, K. M., Green, C., Johnson, C. and McFadden, L., 2007. Evolving concepts in flood risk management: searching for a common language. *Flood Risk Management in Europe: Innovation in Policy and Practice*, S. Begum, M. J. F. Stive and J. W. Hall (eds). Springer, Dordrecht.

de Moel, H., van Alphen, J. and Aerts, J. C. J. H., 2009. Flood maps in Europe – methods, availability and use. *Natural Hazards and Earth System Sciences*, 9(2). 289–301.

Dlugolecki, A. F., 2000. Climate change and the insurance industry. *The Geneva Papers on Risk and Insurance – Issues and Practice*, 25(4). 582–601.

Dlugolecki, A. F., 2008. Climate change and the insurance sector. *The Geneva Papers on Risk and Insurance – Issues and Practice*, 33(1). 71–90.

Downton, M. W. and Pielke, R. A., 2001. Discretion without accountability: politics, flood damage and climate. *Natural Hazards Review*, 2(4). 157–166.

Elsner, J. B., Kossin, J. P. and Jagger, T. H., 2008. The increasing intensity of the strongest tropical cyclones. *Nature*, 455(7209). 92–95.

Emanuel, K., 2005. Increasing destructiveness of tropical cyclones over the past 30 years. *Nature*, 436(7051). 686–688.

Finucane, M. L., Alhakami, A., Slovic, P. and Johnson, S. M., 2000. The affect heuristic in judgements of risks and benefits. *Journal of Behavioral Decision Making*, 13. 1–17.

Flynn, J., Slovic, P., Mertz, C. K. and Carlisle, C., 1999. Public support for earthquake risk mitigation in Portland, Oregon. *Risk Analysis*, 19(2). 205–216.

Freeman, P. K. and Kunreuther, H., 2003. Managing environmental risk through insurance. *The International Yearbook of Environmental and Resource Economics 2003/2004*, H. Folmer and T. Tietenberg (eds). Edward Elgar Publishing, Northampton, UK.

Freeman, P. K., Keen, M. and Mani, M., 2003. *Dealing with Increased Risk of Natural Disasters: Challenges and Options*. IMF Working Paper WP/03/197. International Monetary Fund, Washington, DC.

Godschalk, D., 2003. Urban hazard mitigation: creating resilient cities. *Natural Hazards Review*, 4(3). 136–143.

Grossi, P. and Kunreuther, H. C., 2005. *Catastrophe Modeling: A New Approach of Managing Risk*. Springer, New York.

Handmer, J. W. and Dovers, S. R., 1996. A typology of resilience: rethinking institutions for sustainable development. *Organization & Environment*, 9(4). 482–511.

Heimann, M. and Reichstein, M., 2008. Terrestrial ecosystem, carbon dynamics and climate feedbacks. *Nature*, 451(7176). 289–292.

Hoff, H., Warner, K. and Bouwer, L. M., 2005. The role of financial services in climate adaptation in developing countries. *Vierteljahrshefte zur Wirtschaftsforschung*, 74(2). 196–207.

Holling, C. S., 1973. Resilience and stability of ecological systems. *Annual Review of Ecology and Systematics*, 4(1). 1–23.

Holling, C. S., 1986. The resilience of terrestrial ecosystems: local surprise and global change. *Sustainable Development of the Biosphere*, W. C. Clark and R. E. Munn (eds). Cambridge University Press, Cambridge, UK.

Höppe, P. and Pielke, R., 2006. *Report of the Workshop on Climate Change and Disaster Losses*, October. Hohenkammer, Germany.

Hoyos, C. D., Agudelo, P. A., Webster, P. J. and Curry, J. A., 2006. Deconvolution of the factors contributing to the increase in global hurricane intensity. *Science*, 312(5769). 94–97.

IFRC, 2001. *World Disasters Report*. International Federation of Red Cross and Red Crescent Societies, Geneva.

IPCC (Intergovernmental Panel on Climate Change), 2007. *Climate Change 2007: The Physical Science Basis. Contribution of Working Group I to the Fourth Assessment Report of the Intergovernmental Panel on Climate Change.* S. Solomon, D. Qin, M. Manning, Z. Chen, M. Marquis, K. Averyt, M. M. B. Tignor and H. L. Miller (eds). Cambridge University Press, Cambridge and New York.

Janssen, L. H. J. M., Okker, V. R. and Schuur, J., 2006. Welvaart en leefomgeving: een scenariostudie voor Nederland in 2040. *Achtergronddocument.* Centraal Planbureau, Milieu- en Natuurplanbureau and Ruimtelijk Planbureau. www.welvaartenleefom geving.nl/ (in Dutch).

Jonkman, S. N., Brinkhuis-Jak, M. and Kok, M., 2004. Cost benefit analysis and flood damage mitigation in the Netherlands. *HERON*, 49(1). 95–111.

Kahneman, D., 2003. Maps of bounded rationality: psychology for behavioral economics. *The American Economic Review*, 93(5). 1449–1475.

Kahneman, D. and Tversky, A., 1979. Prospect theory: an analysis of decision under risk. *Econometrica*, 47(2). 263–291.

Kahneman, D., Slovic, P. and Tversky, A., 1982. *Judgment under Uncertainty: Heuristics and Biases.* Cambridge University Press, New York.

Keller, C., Siegrist, M. and Gutscher, H., 2006. The role of the affect and availability heuristics in risk communication. *Risk Analysis*, 26(3). 631–639.

Kennedy, M., Mrofka, D. and von der Borch, C., 2008. Snowball earth termination by destabilization of equatorial permafrost methane clathrate. *Nature*, 453(7195). 642–645.

Kerr, R. A., 2006. A tempestuous birth of hurricane climatology. *Science*, 312(5774). 676–678.

Klein, R. J. T., Nicholls, R. J. and Thomalla, F., 2003. Resilience to natural hazards: how useful is this concept? *Environmental Hazards*, 5(1–2). 35–45.

Kleindorfer, P. and Kunreuther, H. C., 1999. The complementary roles of mitigation and insurance in managing catastrophic risks. *Risk Analysis*, 19(4). 721–732.

Kreibich, H., Thieken, A. H., Petrow, T., Müller, M. and Merz, B., 2005. Flood loss reduction of private households due to building precautionary measures: lessons learned from the Elbe flood in August 2002. *Natural Hazards and Earth System Sciences*, 5(1). 117–126.

Kunreuther, H. C., 1996. Mitigating disaster losses through insurance. *Journal of Risk and Uncertainty*, 12(2–3). 171–187.

Kunreuther, H. C., 2006a. Disaster mitigation and insurance: learning from Katrina. *Annals of the American Academy of Political and Social Science*, 604(1). 208–227.

Kunreuther, H. C., 2006b. Has the time come for comprehensive natural disaster insurance? *On Risk and Disaster: Lessons from Hurricane Katrina*, R. J. Daniels, D. F. Kettl and H. Kunreuther (eds). University of Pennsylvania Press, Philadelphia, PA.

Kunreuther, H. C. and Michel-Kerjan, E. O., 2007. Climate change, insurability of large-scale disasters, and the emerging liability challenge. *University of Pennsylvania Law Review*, 155(6). 1795–1842.

Kunreuther, H. C. and Pauly, M., 2006. Rules rather than discretion: lessons from Hurricane Katrina. *Journal of Risk and Uncertainty*, 33(1). 101–116.

Kunreuther, H. C., Michel-Kerjan, E. O., Doherty, N. A., Grace, M. F., Klein, R. W. and Pauly, M. V., 2008. *Managing Large-Scale Risks in a New Era of Catastrophes: Insuring, Mitigating and Financing Recovery from Natural Disasters in the United States.* Wharton Risk Management and Decision Processes Center, Georgia State University and Insurance Information Institute, Philadelphia, PA.

Landsea, C. W., Harper, B. A., Hoarau, K. and Knaff, J. A., 2006. Can we detect trends in extreme tropical cyclones? *Science*, 313(5786). 452–454.

Lay, T., Kanamori, H., Ammon, C. J., Nettles, M., Ward, S. N., Aster, R. C., Beck, S. L., Bilek, S. L., Brudzinski, M. R., Butler, R., DeShon, H. R., Ekström, G., Satake, K. and Sipkin, S., 2005. The great Sumatra–Andaman earthquake of 26 December 2004. *Science*, 308(5725). 1127–1133.

Loewenstein, G. F., Hsee, C. K., Weber, E. U. and Welch, N., 2001. Risk as feelings. *Psychological Bulletin*, 127(2). 267–286.

Luechinger, S. and Raschky, P. A., 2009. Valuing flood disasters using the life satisfaction approach. *Journal of Public Economics*, 93(3–4). 620–632.

Mason, C. F., Shogren, J. F., Settle, C. and List, J. A., 2005. Investigating risky choices over losses using experimental data. *Journal of Risk and Uncertainty*, 31(2). 187–215.

Merz, B., Kreibich, H., Thieken, A. H. and Schmidtke, R., 2004. Estimation uncertainty of direct monetary flood damage to buildings. *Natural Hazards and Earth System Sciences*, 4(1). 153–163.

Michaels, P., 2006. Is the sky really falling? A review of recent global warming scare stories. *Policy Analysis*, 576. 1–25.

Michel-Kerjan, E. and de Marcellis-Warin, N., 2006. Public–private programs for covering extreme events: the impact of information distribution on risk-sharing. *Asia-Pacific Journal of Risk and Insurance*, 1(2). 21–49.

Michel-Kerjan, E. and Morlaye, F., 2008. Extreme events, global warming, and insurance-linked securities: how to trigger the 'tipping point'. *Geneva Papers on Risk and Insurance – Issues and Practice*, 33(1). 153–176.

Miller, S., Muir-Wood, R. and Boissonnade, A., 2008. An exploration of trends in normalized weather-related catastrophe losses. *Climate Extremes and Society*, H.F. Diaz and R.J. Murnane (eds). Cambridge University Press, Cambridge, UK. 225–247.

Mills, E., 2005. Insurance in a climate of change. *Science*, 309(5737). 1040–1044.

Mills, E., 2007. *From Risk to Opportunity: 2007 – Insurers Responses to Climate Change*. Ceres Report, October. Ceres, Boston, MA.

Mills, E. and Lecomte, E., 2006. *From Risk to Opportunity: How Insurers Can Proactively and Profitably Manage Climate Change*. Ceres Report, August. Ceres, Boston, MA.

Mills, E., Lecomte, E. and Peara, A., 2002. Insurers in the greenhouse. *Journal of Insurance Regulation*, 21(1). 43–78.

Mitchell, R. C. and Carson, R. T., 1989. *Using Surveys to Value Public Goods: The Contingent Valuation Method*. Resources for the Future, Washington, DC.

Muir-Wood, R., Miller, S. and Boissonade, A., 2006. The search for trends in a global catalogue of normalized weather-related catastrophe losses. *Workshop on Climate Change and Disaster Losses*, P. Höppe and R. A. Jr. Pielke, (eds). Hohenkammer, Germany.

Munich Re, 2009. *Topics Geo Natural Catastrophes 2008: Analyses, Assessments, Positions*. Munich Re Group, Munich.

Peacock, W. G., Brody, S. D. and Highfield, W., 2005. Hurricane risk perceptions among Florida's single family homeowners. *Landscape and Urban Planning*, 73(2–3). 120–135.

Pelling, M., 2003. *The Vulnerability of Cities: Natural Disasters and Social Resilience*. Earthscan, London.

Pielke, R. A., Prins, G., Rayner, S. and Sarewitz, D., 2007. Lifting the taboo on adaptation. *Nature*, 445(7128). 597–598.

Pielke, R. A., Gratz, J., Landsea, C. W., Collins, D., Saunders, M. and Musulin, R., 2008. Normalized hurricane damages in the United States: 1900–2005. *Natural Hazards Review*, 9. 29–42.

Pierrehumbert, R. T., 2004. Warming the world. *Nature*, 432(7018). 677.

Pimm, S. L., 1984. The complexity and stability of ecosystems. *Nature*, 307(5949). 321–326.

Porfiriev, B., 2009. Community resilience and vulnerability to disasters: qualitative models and megacities: a comparison with small towns. *Environmental Hazards*, 8(1). 23–37.

Priest, G. L., 1996. The government, the market, and the problem of catastrophic loss. *Journal of Risk and Uncertainty*, 12(2–3). 219–237.

Quiggin, J., 1982. A note on the existence of a competitive optimum. *Economic Record*, 55(161). 174–176.

Rapley, C., 2006. The Antarctic ice sheet and sea level rise. *Avoiding Dangerous Climate Change*, H. J. Schellnhuber, W. Cramer, N. Nakicenovic, T. Wigley and G. Yohe (eds). Cambridge University Press, Cambridge, UK.

Rose, A., 2003. A typology of economic disruptions. *50th Annual North American Meetings of the Regional Science Association International*. Philadelphia, PA.

Rose, A., 2004a. Defining and measuring economic resilience to disasters. *Disaster Prevention and Management*, 13(4). 307–314.

Rose, A., 2004b. Economic principles, issues, and research priorities in hazard loss estimation. *Modelling Spatial and Economic Impacts of Disasters*, Y. Okuyama and S.E. Chang (eds). Springer-Verlag, Berlin and New York.

Rose, A., 2006. Economic resilience to disasters: toward a consistent and comprehensive formulation. *Disaster Resilience: An Integrated Approach*, D. Paton and D. M. Johnson (eds). Charles C. Thomas, New York.

Rose, A., 2007. Economic resilience to natural and man-made disasters: multidisciplinary origins and contextual dimensions. *Environmental Hazards*, 7(4). 383–398.

Saunders, M. A. and Lea, A. S., 2008. Large contribution of sea surface warming to recent increase in Atlantic hurricane activity. *Nature*, 451(7178). 557–560.

Schmeidler, D., 1989. Subjective probability and expected utility without additivity. *Econometrica*, 57(3). 571–587.

Schmidt, S., Kemfert, C. and Höppe, P., 2009. The impact of socio-economics and climate change on tropical cyclone losses in the USA. *Regional Environmental Change*. doi10-1007/s10113-008-0082-4.

Slovic, P., 1987. Perception of risk. *Science*, 236(4799). 280–285.

Slovic, P., 2000. *Perceptions of Risk*. Earthscan, London.

Slovic, P., Finucane, M. L., Peters, E. and MacGregor, D. G., 2004. Risk as analysis and risk as feelings: some thoughts about affect, reason, risk, and rationality. *Risk Analysis*, 24(2). 311–322.

Stern, N., 2007. *The Economics of Climate Change: The Stern Review*. Cambridge University Press, Cambridge, UK.

Thieken, A. H., Müller, M., Kreibich, H. and Merz, B., 2005. Flood damage and influencing factors: new insights from the August 2002 flood in Germany. *Water Resources Research*, 41(12). 1–16.

Thieken, A. H., Petrow, T., Kreibich, H. and Merz, B., 2006. Insurability and mitigation of flood losses in private households in Germany. *Risk Analysis*, 26(2). 383–395.

Timmerman, P., 1981. *Vulnerability, Resilience and the Collapse of Society: A Review of Models and Possible Climatic Applications*. Institute for Environmental Studies, University of Toronto, Toronto.

Tobin, G. A., 1999. Sustainability and community resilience: the Holy Grail of natural hazards planning? *Environmental Hazards*, 1(1). 13–25.

Tversky, A. and Kahneman, D., 1992. Advances in prospect theory: cumulative representation of uncertainty. *Journal of Risk and Uncertainty*, 5(4). 297–323.

van Dantzig, D., 1956. Economic decision problems for flood prevention. *Econometrica*, 24(3). 276–287.

Vellinga, P., Mills, E., Berz, G., Bouwer, L. M., Huq, S., Kozak, L. A., Palutikof, J., Schanzenbächer, B. and Soler, G., 2001. Insurance and other financial services (Chapter 8). *Climate Change 2001: Impacts, Adaptation, and Vulnerability*, J. J. McCarthy, O. F. Canziani, N. A. Leary, D. J. Dokken and S. White (eds). Cambridge University Press, Cambridge, UK. 417–450.

Vis, M., Klijn, F., de Bruijn, K. M. and van Buuren, M., 2003. Resilience strategies for flood risk management in the Netherlands. *The International Journal of River Basin Management*, 1(1). 33–40.

von Neumann, J. and Morgenstern, O., 1947. *The Theory of Games and Economic Behavior* (2nd edn). Princeton University Press, Princeton, NJ.

von Ungern-Sternberg, T., 2009. *Hurricane Insurance in Florida*. Seminar paper, Adaptation to Climate Change: The Role of Insurance. Innsbruck, Austria.

Webster, P. J., Holland, G. J., Curry, J. A. and Chang, H. R., 2005. Changes in tropical cyclone number, duration, and intensity in a warmer environment. *Science*, 309(5742). 1844–1846.

Wood, R., Collins, M., Gregory, J., Harris, G. and Vellinga, M., 2006. Towards a risk assessment for the shutdown of the Atlantic Thermohaline Circulation. *Avoiding Dangerous Climate Change*, H. J. Schellnhuber, W. Cramer, N. Nakicenovic, T. Wigley and G. Yohe (eds). Cambridge University Press, Cambridge, UK.

ENVIRONMENTAL
HAZARDS
Human and Policy Dimensions

Responsibility framing in a 'climate change induced' compounded crisis: Facing tragic choices in the Murray–Darling Basin

EVA-KARIN OLSSON*

Crismart/Swedish National Defence College, Drottning Kristinas väg 37, Box 27805, 115 93 Stockholm, Sweden

Crises impose vast demands on political leaders' communicative abilities in terms of explaining the causes of the problem at hand as well as showing a plausible way out of the situation. These challenges become even more complex in connection with climate change induced compounded crises. These crises touch upon a broad range of issues, such as economic, environmental, social and energy policies. Drawing upon previous research on political crisis communication, this article aims to examine political actors framing strategies in connection with compounded crises and how these are affected by the media context in which they are communicated. The study rests on a case study examining *The Australian*'s reporting of the drought in the Murray–Darling Basin in terms of how various actor groups portrayed in the reporting framed crisis responsibility. The article ends by proposing propositions for further research on responsibility framing in climate change induced compounded crises.

Keywords: climate change; crisis communication; drought; environmental communication; responsibility framing

1. Introduction

According to Beck (2002, p. 41) the world risk society is facing three fundamental conflicts or predicaments: global financial crises, global terror networks and ecological conflicts. Even though crisis communication scholars have acknowledged the role of political communication and 'meaning making' in acute crises (see, for example, Boin et al., 2005), research has only begun to address communication challenges posed by new types of transnational and compounded crises such as terrorism (Norris et al., 2003; Papacharissi and de Fatima Oliveira, 2008); pandemics (Buus and Olsson, 2006; Shih et al., 2008; Ungar, 2008) and climate change (McComas and Shanahan, 1999; Weingart et al., 2000; Berglez, 2008; Olsson and Paglia, 2008). This article aims to add to the growing literature by examining *responsibility framing* in connection with the media coverage of the prevailing crisis in the Murray–Darling Basin in Australia during

2008, as an example of a 'climate change induced' compounded crisis inheriting ecological, social, economic and political predicaments. The historic drought affecting Australia is sometimes said to be the developed world's first climate change crisis. As a drought-prone country with massive fossil fuel resources, and with important economic sectors such as agriculture and tourism vulnerable to climate shifts, Australia stands to lose from both the effects of climate change and any measures aimed at mitigation through carbon limitations. Besides the longer-term effects of climate change, the drought is at the same time an acute crisis in its own right, with three million Australians directly depending on its water. However, a prolonged drought in the area does not only have economic and social effects at the local level but also at the national level where the agriculture industry depending on the Basin is worth more than AUD9 billion per annum (www.environment.gov.au/water/mdb/index.html).

■ *E-mail:* eva-karin.olsson@fhs.se

ENVIRONMENTAL HAZARDS 8 (2009) 226–240

doi:10.3763/ehaz.2009.0019 © 2009 Earthscan ISSN: 1747-7891 (print), 1878-0059 (online) www.earthscanjournals.com

In relation to crisis management, compounded crises are of special interest, as noted by Porfiriev (2000), since they override the dichotomy between slow-burning (see, for example, 't Hart and Boin, 2001) and fast-burning crises (which has been the main focus in crisis management studies). The melting together of risk and crisis is also evident in the media coverage of climate change, where research in the field has demonstrated how the discourse on climate change has moved beyond its previous occupation with scientific certainty/uncertainty into a more traditional political discourse, forcing political leaders to take a clear stance on global warming (Weingart et al., 2000; Andreadis and Smith, 2007).

> We are entering a period when careful interpretation and communication of the economic, political and social dimensions of climate change will be vital. Failure to tell these aspects of the story could have even greater significance than the painfully slow arrival at the basics of science (Andreadis and Smith, 2007, p. 53).

This basically means that leaders have to be able to communicate a phenomenon that is in essence scientific, global in its nature and non-visible in its appearance. As argued by Beck (2005), in order to tell the story of ecological predicaments these invisible and slow changes have to be attached to visible and measured 'impacts', which often need a cultural resonance. The need to attach invisible risks looming in the future to concrete events is also evident in the reporting of climate change, which has been found to correlate with increased temperatures (Ungar, 1992; McComas and Shanahan, 1999), peak events such as the 1997 Kyoto conference (Krosnick et al., 1998), or extreme weather events (Weingart et al., 2000). In describing extreme weather events as 'critical discourse moments', Carvalho and Burgess (2005, p. 1466) point to the crucial role they play for media coverage of global warming, which changed the whole discourse in 1999–2000 when it became attached to a new sense of urgency. The general sense of urgency in today's environmental media coverage is also what makes Cox (2007) call for the understanding of environmental communication as a 'crisis discipline'. Taken together, these calls and findings motivate the study of 'climate change induced' crises from a communicative perspective. However, the blurring of the traditional distinction between slow- and fast-burning crises poses the question of whether compounded crises can accurately be examined by applying traditional theories in the field. In line with this, the article at hand is an attempt to modify and discuss crisis communication theories, focusing on responsibility framing in connection with a 'climate change induced' compounded crisis.

The starting point is that compounded crises challenge the foundations of crisis communication theories which have been developed based on a notion of crises as the consequence of a single cause, confined to one organization, characterized by a clear beginning and end (Seeger et al., 2003, pp. 86–87). Turning to the research on political crisis communication, there is a similar tendency to focus exclusively on rhetorical devices applied by political actors, at the expense of other stakeholders such as business and various interest groups, when communicating in an acute crisis (see, for example, Brändström and Kuipers, 2003; de Vries, 2004; Brändström et al., 2008). In line with this, previous literature has shown a general lack of research that takes into account the general media context in which the framing contest takes place (Hallahan, 1999; Ihlen and Nitz, 2008). This is troublesome, given the extensive bulk of research showing that the media play a pivotal role in society's framing of political issues (Goffman, 1974; Graber, 1988; 1993; Edelman, 1988; McLeod et al., 1994; Semetko and Valkenburg, 2000; Entman, 2003). The article bridges the two research traditions in examining responsibility framing in a media context, taking into account all actors involved in the 'framing contest' (see Gamson and Stuart, 1992; Wolfsfeld, 1998; Gamson, 2004; Boin et al., 2008). Based on the notion of framing contests, this article then aims to examine political actors framing strategies in compounded crises and how these are affected by the media context in which they are communicating. In drawing upon previous literature in the field, the following research questions have guided the study: how and by whom are the situation, its causes and solutions framed? Based on the analysis, the article ends by proposing propositions for further research on responsibility framing in 'climate change induced' compounded crises.

1.1. Responsibility framing

In general, framing theory can be seen as a combination of different aspects of content analyses, ranging from agenda setting to discourse theory. The power of frames depends on their ability to categorize and connect bits of information into a coherent whole (Gamson, 1992). Frames can be studied at different levels of detail, where scholars such as Semetko and Valkenburg (2000) and Iyengar (1991) argue for the study of so-called meta-frames. This article does not examine the meta-framing of the drought but concentrates on various frames applied by actor groups quoted in the coverage. In line with Gurevitch and Levy (1985, p.19) framing is here understood as a contest or power struggle between different actors where media perform a vital function in acting as a battlefield for politicians, social groups, institutions and ideologies. Media research on responsibility framing has traditionally focused on common overarching frames employed by journalists such as: *diagnostic* frames (which identify the problem and diagnose the cause of the problem); *prognostic* frames (which provide information on what ought to be done); and *motivation* frames (which suggest remedies) (Gamson, 1992; Gerhards and Rucht, 1992; Entman, 2003). An underlying notion of all three frames is journalists' power to assign legitimacy to actors. This process can be thought of in terms of 'status conferral', which means that journalists mediate status to actors by connecting them with certain issues and values. Simonson (1999, p. 109) states that 'Via the status conferral function, media contribute

to the social process of confidence by boosting the public standing of the ideas, institutions, and people they portray.'

Moving away from media research, crisis communication scholars take the perspective of crisis managers, particularly political actors ('t Hart, 1993; Brändström and Kuipers, 2003; Boin et al., 2008) or corporate actors (Marcus and Goodman, 1991; Siomkos and Shrivastava, 1993; Coombs, 1998; 2007; Massey, 2001; Coombs and Holladay, 2002) when studying communication. Generally speaking, this strand of research tends to regard crisis communication as a game, eventually won by the actor applying the most successful rhetorical devices. Following Boin et al. (2005), one of the primary tasks for leaders in a crisis situation is to explain the situation and to justify actions taken, so-called meaning making. In order to be successful, leaders must be 'communicating a persuasive story line (a narrative) that explains what happened, why it had to be that way, what its repercussions are, how it can be resolved, who can be relied upon and who is to blame' (Boin et al., 2005, p. 70). In order to win the 'blame game' over political opponents, decisions along the following three lines have to be made: how severe is the crisis, how could it happen, and who is responsible.

Managers in general strive to frame the crisis as a natural event, allowing it to be placed outside the scope of political responsibility. The worse possible outcome would be if the crisis is framed as caused by political leaders (on a personal or policy level) (Brändström and Kuipers, 2003; de Vries, 2004). Due to the erosion of the traditional distinction between crises as 'man-made' and 'acts of God', establishing crisis causes is to a large extent a question of the actors' framing ability (Rosenthal et al., 2001, p. 6). According to Beck (2002, p. 40), if 'pre-modern dangers were attributed to nature, gods and demons risks in modern times are rather about control and political decision-making'. Following this, 'nature' has moved from being understood as an uncontrollable force to an object that can be controlled by scientific and technological advances (Dear, 2006). It should thus be noted that some crises are more suitable for blame games, such as wars, which have an inherent potential for enemy constructions, whereas compounded and structural problems (such as economic recessions or environmental problems) are less suitable for blame games and responsibility framing (Edelman, 1988). This is because they are harder to explain by personal and straightforward causes, which complicate political attacks or crisis exploitation. On the contrary, political actors are often tempted to downplay the problems, and thereby in the long run risk coming off as paralysed (Edelman, 1988, p. 82). According to Beck (2002), the fundamental problem in ascribing liability in connection to financial or ecological crises is that they 'are mainly due to the combined effects of the actions of many individuals' (Beck, 2002, p. 41). It should also be noted that the framing of the event as severe does not necessarily pose a threat to political actors but might well be an opportunity to show action and to push through a new set of policies (see Boin et al., 2009 on 'crisis exploitation').

In this article I examine various actors' framing as played out in the media. Journalistic framing of an issue is one very significant factor that influences actors' framing opportunities. When the media give prominent coverage to certain actors, in the end it greatly affects the possible positions for the other actors. The framing contest around the Murray–Darling crisis will be examined by applying the three dimensions pivotal to responsibility framing, i.e. how severe is the crisis, how could it happen and who is responsible. However, in contrast to previous research on crisis communication, the framework will be applied to the media coverage as a whole, including all groups of actors.

1.2. Analytical framework

For a start, framing severity relates to the framing of the situation as such, in terms of its character. As stressed by Boin et al. (2005) there is a vital difference in labelling a situation as an incident,

an accident, a crisis, a disaster or a tragedy (p. 83). In connection to climate change induced crises, Olsson and Paglia (2008) show that severity framing requires actors to position themselves on a scale of uncertainty/certainty in relation to causes and outcomes, and that despite scientific uncertainty, political actors are forced to take a stance on the issue. This frame is important since how an event is labelled has significant implications for the proposal of potential solutions; that is, whether a top-priority or a simple routine response is issued (Boin et al., 2009).

Framing the nature of the crisis is further closely connected to the second aspect in the framework, that is, where to locate the origin of the event which, according to previous research on responsibility framing, is pivotal for assigning responsibility. Accordingly, so-called blame games depend on the actors' ability to ascribe the crisis to exogenous factors (located outside the realm of the responsible actors) or to endogenous factors (where responsible actors are the very source of the problem). Framing crises as exogenous makes it easier for political actors to make authoritative statements and to remain in control of the information flow, whereas events framed as endogenous run the risk of undermining confidence in actors and of creating an opening for criticism (Coombs, 1998; 2007; Massey, 2001, p. 158; Coombs and Holladay, 2002; Boin et al., 2008; Brändström et al., 2008).

From a political perspective, a crisis does not end with leader's communicative devices in terms of accepting (or not) responsibility for what has happened but also requires an ability to show a way out of the current problems. Political crisis communication will therefore not only be a blame game but also an opportunity game, where actors have to play the delicate game of matching their labelling of the event to adequate policies. As with the other two themes, we can expect a variety of actors to engage in proposing solutions. As argued by Boin et al. (2008), actors get involved under different conditions where actors without the power to actually implement the proposed policies have more freedom to come up with solutions, in contrast to governmental actors. Governmental representatives further have to balance between proposing solutions and reassurance that the system is solid in essence. Three potential outcomes can be expected in the policy game: 'fine tuning', which means instrumental and incremental adaptations without any change of political values; 'policy reform', which relates to major policy principles being changed that otherwise would be hard to change under normal circumstances; and finally 'paradigm shift', which occurs when 'entire policies, organizations or even fundamental normative aspects become subject to abdication' (Boin et al., 2008, p. 17). It should be noted that the aim of the paper is not to examine policy change, but rather the framing of different policy alternatives as they are played out in the media reporting.

2. Methods and material

The paper rests on a case study of how the national Australian newspaper *The Australian* reported the Murray–Darling Basin crisis between 5 August and 31 October 2008. The newspaper was chosen due to its national outlook and reach as a way to examine responsibility framing at the national level (that is, without regional biases). The articles included in the study have been selected from a period when *The Australian* ran a special series under the heading 'Special report: the Murray–Darling crisis'. Altogether 57 newspaper articles were published in this series and each of them has been included in my analysis. The articles have been analysed by a combination of quantitative and qualitative analyses. The quantitative analysis consisted of counting the groups of actors quoted in the news coverage. Based on an inductive approach, actors were coded into five groups which were found to be of relevance to the framing of the crisis. These were governmental actors, federal opposition political actors, state actors, scientists and affected actors (including

individual farmers as well as business interests related to farming and communities in affected areas). It should be noted that actors were only counted once for each article, which means that the measure does not account for the actual space provided to the actors or the number of times an actor was mentioned in one article. The qualitative analysis was deployed in order to describe the main arguments and rhetoric strategies applied by the actor groups. The analysis was conducted by categorizing statements from various actor groups according to the three themes described in the analytical framework. The most important expressions, keywords and key messages were coded, based on Entman's definition of frames: 'the presence or absence of certain keywords, stock phrases, stereotyped images, sources of information and sentences that provide thematically reinforcing clusters of facts and judgments' (Entman, 1993, p. 52). The aim of the analysis was to find common features in how actor groups framed the three themes. Due to the focus on actor groups in the analysis, the framing contest is not primarily understood as taking place within groups, but rather between them.

2.1. Case description

The Murray–Darling Basin is a catchment area for the Murray and Darling rivers and their tributaries. It extends from Queensland to South Australia, including three-quarters of New South Wales and half of Victoria. The basin generates 39 per cent of the national income derived from agriculture production: 53 per cent of Australian cereals grown for grain, 95 per cent of oranges, and 54 per cent of apples. In addition it supports 28 per cent of the nation's cattle herd, 45 per cent of sheep, and 62 per cent of pigs. The Basin is home to more than 2 million residents. In Australia, irrigated land is just 0.6 per cent of total agricultural land and the proportion in the Basin is 2 per cent, making up 65 per cent of Australia's total irrigated agricultural land. Furthermore, the Basin is vital from a natural resource perspective, with extensive wetlands which perform essential hydrological, biological and chemical functions and which support and maintain the productivity and health of the river systems. A number of the Basin wetlands are recognized under the Convention on Wetlands of International Importance. In the last 100 years, life in the Murray–Darling Basin has been transformed by the construction of major water storages on the rivers. The total volume of publicly managed water storage capacity in the Basin is just under 35,000 gigalitres. Of that, the Murray–Darling Basin Authority – with major storages at the Dartmouth Dam, Hume Dam, Lake Victoria, Torrumbarry Weir, the Menindee Lakes and other river regulatory structures – is responsible for about one-third. The storages have made it possible to store water to be released in summer time or in times of drought.

It should be noted that the case is complex because it touches upon broad policy areas involving water management and climate change, policy areas that are highly politicized in the Australian context, and as such involve many twists and turns in which the states depending on the Basin for water supply (New South Wales, Queensland, South Australia, the Australian Capital Territory and Victoria) play a vital role. One example of initiatives undertaken by the Kevin Rudd government to deal with the problems of the Basin is the Murray–Darling Basin Authority (MDBA) established on 15 December 2008, which for the first time ever made one single agency responsible for water management in the Murray–Darling Basin. According to the Water Act 2007, MDBA should prepare a plan in consultation with the Basin states and the communities. The first plan is intended to commence in 2011. The main tasks will be: to limit the amount of water that can be taken from the Basin on a sustainable basis; to identify risks to Basin water resources such as climate change as well as strategies to manage these risks; to make sure that state water resource plans comply with the Act; to follow an environmental watering plan and the salinity management plans; and to comply with rules about trading water rights in

relation to the Basin resources. However, due to the perceived urgency of the problems, the Murray–Darling Basin Program has already been launched. Under the Water for the Future Program, the government has secured AUD21.9 billion to develop more efficient water use by finding new sources of water and to buy back water entitlements from willing sellers (AUD3.1 billion). The main task is to acquire water licenses from willing sellers in order to use the allocated water for the environment. The first AUD50 million water buyback in 2007/2008 aimed to secure 35 billion litres of water, and another was announced on 8 September 2008 in the northern part of the Basin (www.mdba.gov.au/).

3. Empirical analysis

3.1. Framing the situation

First, which actor groups were quoted framing the situation and which frames were deployed? Figure 1 shows the number of quotes made by each of the actor groups in terms of framing the situation (that is, what kind of situation this is). As can be seen from the figure, there were few statements altogether describing the situation (even though many of the scientist quotes were lengthy – at times almost taking up the whole article in question). The most frequently quoted actors were scientists, followed by government and affected actors.

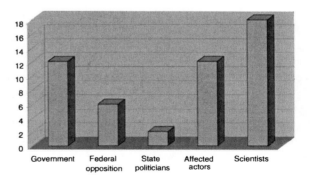

FIGURE 1 Numbers of quotes in the coverage framing the situation distributed across actor groups

How did the actors quoted frame the event? Starting with the scientists, the outlook painted for the Murray–Darling Basin is grim. The terminology used to describe the situation stressed the gravity of the problem, using expressions such as 'ecological disaster', 'crisis', 'collapse', 'one of the major inland problems of our time' and 'tragedy'. The severity of the situation was beyond any doubt. 'It is so far off the scale ecologically that it is a crisis – and that is not overstating it' (*The Australian*, 12 August 2008). 'The river systems and the agriculture systems are collapsing' (*The Australian*, 21 August 2008). Politicians were framed as facing a tragic choice: letting the lower lakes of the river acidify or flooding the lakes with seawater in order to prevent acidification and consequently changing the entire ecosystem. The severity of the situation was further emphasized by the description of decisions as 'irreversible'. The framing of the situation as a tragic choice set the tone of the reporting and underlined both the complexity and the urgency of the situation. The framing, in which available alternatives were all attached to major irreversible changes in ecosystems, posed new challenges to crisis communication insofar as it questioned the traditional underpinning of crisis communication as a means to returning to 'normalcy' (Seeger et al., 2003).[1] Further, the frame underlined the notion of decision making in risk society as based on 'calculating the incalculable' (Beck, 2002, p. 40). This leads us to the question of how the situation was framed by the political actors who had to balance ecological concerns with other societal needs.

The government's assessment of the situation followed the scientific framing in describing the ecological system as 'highly stressed'. No competing views were directly provided by other political actors. As could be seen above, political opponents were not particularly active in framing the situation and when they did, they stressed the underlying risk for the whole ecosystem (emphasizing the need for swift action). However, in contrast to the government, they mentioned the desperate situation for farms and communities affected by the drought – pointing out that there were not only ecosystems in danger but also the livelihoods of the people who depended upon the Basin. For example, the South Australian Premier Mike Rann declared that 'anyone "treacherously" diverting water from the Murray–Darling system illegally would be committing "an act of terrorism against the Australian people"' (*The Australian*, 16 August 2008). The desperation was echoed throughout farming society and interest groups connected to farming. The articles in the sample can be divided into two types: articles describing the effects upon communities at risk of disappearing, and articles depicting individual farmers who had been living on their farms for generations. Examples of the latter category of coverage include: '"Gone from thriving to just surviving" – Ken Brain's property looks a lot different today than it did a decade ago' (*The Australian*, 3 September 2008), and 'Water dries up life on the land – Randall Crozier stands in the barren paddock, frowning at the drought-bleached desert sand' (*The Australian*, 13 September 2008).

To sum up, the scientists were the main actors quoted in framing the severity of the situation, although all quoted actors framed the situation as an urgent crisis. Yet there is an underlining value conflict in the coverage between saving the ecosystem or farming communities where different actors took somewhat different stances. For example, the scientists tended to emphasize the need for reconfiguration of the water allocation systems and the agriculture sectors, whereas the farming communities advocated the loss of towns and businesses in the Murray–Darling area. The politicians were caught in between these two frames, where the tendency for the government was to follow the scientists' framing in terms of reconfiguration of water management systems, whereas the Opposition was more inclined towards framing the situation in favour of affected communities.

3.2. Framing the cause of the event

As discussed in previous sections, the allocation of crisis causes (to exogenous or endogenous factors) is to a large extent a matter of framing, which turns phenomena such as droughts into potential political issues. Figure 2 illustrates the number of quotes made by each of the actor groups in terms of framing the cause of the event.

If politicians were sparsely quoted in framing the situation, they were even less active in framing the causes of the crisis. According to previous research, the framing of causes is the most important factor in the process of politicizing and assigning blame in connection to crises. However, Figure 2 shows that both scientists and affected actors played a major role in framing causes. This might well be an effect of the compounded character of the crisis, which according to Edelman (1988) is harder to explain by personal and simple identified causes.

Starting with politicians, both the government and the opposition framed the crisis as caused by mismanagement of the river system. This reminds me of Beck and Lau's (2005) observation that the recognition of risks as human-made results in political actors being both problem producers and solvers at the same time. In relation to this it is interesting to note that the government emphasized the time perspective in referring to the mismanagement of the Basin. An example is when Kevin Rudd said, 'I do not want to say that there is some magic solution. It is very difficult in the space of six months to turn back decades of neglect' (*The Australian*, 14 August 2008), or when he said, 'I am trying to turn around a situation which has evolved

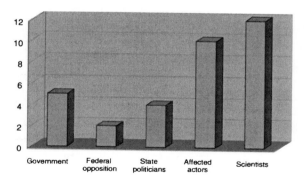

FIGURE 2 Numbers of quotes in the coverage framing the cause(s) of the event distributed across actor groups

over many years' (*The Australian*, 15 August 2008). In doing so, the government tried to downplay expectations by juxtaposing the long history of mismanagement with the acute crisis management expected from the government. Yet they did not downplay the problem as such.

Further, as argued by Olsson and Paglia (2008), a vital component of framing causes in climate change induced crises is the link between climate change and the local/national acute crisis. Actors basically confront two framing options: acknowledging the link to climate change (endogenous factors) or arguing that the drought is caused by nature (exogenous factors). From a political perspective, the latter option would get actors off the responsibility hook, which would then be the preferable outcome for politicians who do not want to (or are unable to, due to previous policies in the area) exploit the crisis (Boin et al., 2009). In this actual case, the government advocated the link between the drought and climate change whereas the then-leader of the opposition Brendan Nelson first denied the link, only to take it back shortly after (saying the two might well be linked but that the debate was irrelevant). However, the reluctant stance towards how to tackle climate change, proposing that Australia should wait with a national emissions trading scheme before international action was taken, was overruled by the Liberal Party, who decided to introduce an Australian emissions scheme in 2012. As a result, Brendan Nelson lost his position to Malcolm Turnbull[2] (*Sydney Morning Herald*, 16 September 2008). On the other hand, ever since it came to power in 2007, the government has been advocating the risk of climate change and in accordance proposed a 'cap and trade system' on carbon dioxide in Australia. Linking the Murray–Darling Basin crisis with climate change would accordingly enhance the government's policies on climate change.

The most heated political debates and blame gaming took place at the state level, among the states depending on the Murray–Darling area for water, rather than at federal level. The state foremost framed as the villain was Queensland, which was blamed for taking too much water out of the system, in particular by South Australia, which was the most badly affected state. As an example, Queensland Water Minister Craig Wallence was quoted as saying, 'pointing the finger at state's irrigators was not going to ease the national emergency' (22 August 2008), whereas South Australian Premier Mike Rann said that even if Queensland irrigators had acted legally, it 'doesn't mean to say it's right' (22 August 2008). In contrast to the scientific framing, the framing among the state politicians as well as the affected groups had more of a practical here-and-now perspective, and the main debate centred around how to distribute water along the river. Many strong opinions were expressed and a fierce blame game was played out in the media where, for example, actors argued that: farmers should not be blamed ('farmers don't have any water', 5 August 2008); or certain states ought to be blamed for taking a disproportional amount of water ('we have significant over-extractions in Queensland', 21 August 2008); or debating the existence of big irrigation farms ('Cubbie was developed in the wrong spot',[3] 22 August 2008). Consequently, the individual states and farmers tried to defend themselves. For example, the rice farmers in their defence pointed the finger back at the government and claimed that 'the area was designed by the government to put food on tables. We went out and did that. We produce the most efficient rice in the world' (*The Australian*, 3 September 2008).

As in framing the character of the crisis, scientists played an important role in framing causes. Interesting to note in relation to the political framing contest over the link with climate change is an article quoting two scientists, one of them the former 'Australian of the Year', Professor Tim Flannery. The two jointly describe, in connection with the political struggle over the link with climate change, the debate as 'fruitless'.

Instead of arguing about this, surely we need to sit down and say: 'What are we going to do if the worst case develops? What we've had is

ten years of catastrophic low flows – what do we do if this is the future?' That's a much more interesting question (Flannery, 4 September 2008).

This quote illustrates the intriguing implications of climate change in connection with responsibility framing where its global nature might lead to apathy at the national level (as suggested by Beck, 2002) and/or lead to politicians getting off the responsibility hook (as suggested by, for example, Brändström and Kuipers, 2003). It should thus be noted that even though the scientists referred to above were pointing to the risk of climate change being taken hostage by the politicians, it should not be read as if the groups of scientists were denying climate change. On the contrary, climate change was in general mentioned as one of the underlying causes, besides a general over-allocation of water and mismanagement of the river system. According to their frame, the mismanagement was caused by the fact that there was no national water management authority (*The Australian*, 21 August 2008) or by the fact that the irrigation structure was simply too big to be supported by the river (*The Australian*, 6 September 2008). Causes were in general framed at the system level, and only on one occasion was blame assigned more directly, which was done in relation to a report published in 2006, calling for 'significant and urgent intervention'. According to one of the quoted authors of the report, 'It is a tragedy that the warning bells that we sounded very loudly way back then were seemingly ignored' (*The Australian*, 12 August 2008). In contrast to political actors, scientists framed the crisis as caused by structural problems such as the lack of a federal water management system and general over-allocation of water. This points to the fact that the more scientists involved in framing a compounded crisis, the less personal blame gaming will take place.

Based on what has been said above, causes were framed in different ways by the actor groups. On the federal level, the only issue touching political nerves was the connection with climate change, whereas the most heated blame game was concentrated at the state level. It thus seems that the closer to the actual problem, the more intense blaming is centred on concrete causes (such as who is taking the most water) rather than more complex structural problems (such as global warming or a total overhaul of the irrigation system).

3.3. Framing measures

The last frame deals with the actions taken and proposed by the actors. As can be seen in Figure 3, this is the frame that received most media coverage. In contrast to the two other themes explored above, the affected groups were the most frequently quoted actor group, followed by the government, closely followed by scientists.

As is evident from the figure, this was the frame that caught the most intense media attention. The debate was, in general, focused on the government's two main propositions to deal with the crisis: the Water Act and the Murray–Darling Basin Program. The framing from the government's perspective, except for promoting actions taken in the area, was to downplay expectations by stressing the lack of 'magic solutions' (*The Australian*, 14 August 2008). As discussed in the previous section, one main aspect of how to cope with the event was to link the drought with climate change. Denying the link enabled

the handling of the crisis with acute operational measures. On the other hand, acknowledging the link implied the need for long-term system changes. In relation to this, the government tried to use the crisis in order to promote their policies on water management in the Murray–Darling area as well as the Cap and Trade Carbon Pollution Reduction Scheme.[4] Even though policies applied by the government in the area 'fitted' into the framing of both the situation (crisis) as well as its causes (mismanagement and climate change), they were not uncontested by other actors. On the contrary, this was the theme that provoked the most heated political debate.

In contrast to the other two frames, the debate had a technical overtone and focused on moves and statements made by different actors. In fact, the reporting was very much in line with the media's well-documented tendency to portray politics as a game, focusing on conflicts and often describing them in sporting metaphors (Fallows, 1996; Jamieson, 2001). From an environmental communication perspective, Ihlen and Nitz (2008) concluded, on the basis of a Norwegian case study, that media coverage was heavily dominated by tensions between actors and so-called 'horse race frames'. Their conclusions very much resembled the debate in this frame where the main bulk of the reporting focused on the government's proposed measures to deal with the problem and criticism from other actors. Scientists, opposition and affected groups argued that the buyback scheme (referring to the government's initiative to buy back water entitlements) was ineffective. Likewise, the opposition made an issue out of the fact that they did not trust the government's estimation of how much water there was in the system and called for an inquiry. The government countered by saying that people wanted action and did not want an inquiry. For example, the scientists criticized the buyback scheme for being 'insignificant' and claimed that it would 'do nothing for the Coorong'.[5] In a similar manner, the federal opposition argued that the buyback was 'paper money' that only risked 'destroying communities'. Again

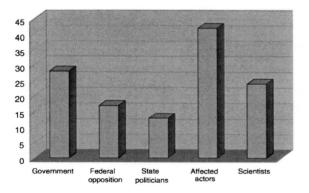

FIGURE 3 Numbers of quotes in the coverage framing measures distributed across actor groups

this was echoed by the affected actors saying that the government was 'buying water entitlements not actual water'. The group of affected actors was also blaming the government for ignoring the broader impact of their policies:

> Wouldn't it be a tragedy if people in town weren't paid. If the farmer is paid to leave, there would be no town. So it would just be a ridiculous proposition to buy out the farmers and not buy out the town (2 September, 2008).

In summary, it can be noted that this was the most politicized frame of all, going against previous research primarily pointing out the causes of the crisis to be the frame determining politicization in crisis. One reason might well be that the scientists, who in the two other frames were allowed to make authoritative claims when defining the situation and its causes, had a less strong role in this frame, thus opening up more of a competition among other actors' framing.

4. Discussion

The article has illustrated that responsibility framing in connection with compounded crises can significantly gain by considering not only political actors' framing of a situation but also those other actor groups involved in framing a crisis. Such an approach will provide a richer understanding of constraints and opportunities facing various actors. One conclusion to be drawn from the analysis is that crisis managers are facing basically two types of constraints affecting their 'communicative spaces': external media factors (actors' own previous policies in related areas) and internal media factors (other actors' framing of the issue as it plays out in the media). Actors are in general in control of the first one (in which they are rather bound by their own previous policy commitments), whereas the latter depends on media coverage of a particular event. Before moving on to the propositions derived from the case in relation to further research on communication in compounded crises, it should be noted that this

discussion was based on a single case study and that additional studies are needed in order to further develop the general propositions below.

Starting with the external aspect affecting actors' communicative spaces, the case is a good example of the coupling mechanism between a concrete crisis and climate change that gives 'climate change induced' compounded crises certain characteristics (see also Olsson and Paglia, 2008). In this case, the coupling between the actual crisis and related policies urges crisis communication research to move outside the domains of the crisis at hand by taking into consideration the broader policymaking context. In relation to the focus on single crisis communicative settings in previous research, communicators in compounded crises run the risk of having a particular crisis contaminated by related policy issues, which limit the actors' communicative options. Or, from the other perspective, it can be used to strengthen their case. It reminds me of what Boin et al. (2009) refer to as 'crisis exploitation', which means that political actors can exploit crises in order to push through their pet policies. In order for actors to be trustworthy, they need to be consistent. In this case, that means not only communicating in the actual crisis but also in relation to what has been said and done prior to the crisis in areas that are now being linked to the crisis. This explains why the government made the link between the Murray–Darling crisis and climate change, whereas the opposition first tried to downplay the link. In summary, previous policy commitments framed as being linked to the crisis at hand will both enable and constrain the actors' ability to communicate.

4.1. Proposition one: The communicative space provided to political actors will be affected by previous policies proposed in area(s) framed as being linked to the acute crisis

As already argued, not only external policy commitments but also media aspects will have an impact on political actors' crisis communication options. This is so because media coverage of crises consists of a variety of actors involved in framing the event. In the actual case, the scientists and affected actors were given considerable space on all three framing themes. As argued by previous researchers in the field (Weingart et al., 2000; Andreadis and Smith, 2007), climate change coverage has moved beyond its previous occupation with scientific uncertainty into being reported as foremost a political issue. However, as can be seen in the empirical analysis, this does not mean that scientists are not participating in the debate. On the contrary, it can be argued that scientists' framing power becomes even stronger when there is a consensus on a particular issue, since it poses limitations on other actors' framing options. The fact that the opposition leader Brendan Nelson came under heavy criticism for denying the link points to another important aspect here, that the link between climate change and extreme weather events has become stronger, up to the point where it simply cannot be questioned. Together, the discussion above stresses the notion that political actors are constrained by the societal and political discourse in which they communicate. Given the strong role of scientists quoted in the news coverage, it seems fair to argue that other actors had less space in framing the issue, as illustrated in the figures in this analysis, in connection with framing the severity of the crisis and its causes. These two factors are vital to responsibility framing since they limit the range of potential measures aimed at curbing the crisis. On a more specific level, there were also examples of when scientists spoke more directly to politicians. They were then acting in the capacity of 'frame guards' determined by how other actors ought to frame the crisis. One example was when the scientists urged the political actors to stop arguing over the link between the drought and climate change for fear that the climate change issue risked taking over the debate and being used as an excuse for inaction. The second proposition is then that the participation of other actors in the media coverage had an impact on the political actors' communicative spaces.

More specifically, in relation to 'climate change induced' crises, we can expect scientists to play an important role in framing the situation and its causes.

4.2. Proposition two: The strong role of scientists in framing crisis severity and causes limits political actors' framing options

Except for scientists, the second most frequently quoted group was 'affected actors', especially when it came to framing concrete measures. It might well be the case that interest groups always play a prominent role in framing measures in relation to crises, but their strong presence in this case might likewise rest on the specific cultural Australian context in which farmers and rural communities have a strong cultural symbolic and economic value. As argued by Goffman (1981, p. 63), frames are culturally grounded, making them 'a central part of a culture'. According to Botterill (2003), drought has to be understood as a social construction and as such highly political in its nature. However, as argued by West and Smith (1996), drought is a national symbol of Australia, which means that in contrast to climate change, drought policies have not been a politically sensitive issue in Australia, and have not been questioned in the media debate. Rather, the 'bush' and the rural areas have been presented as quintessentially Australian – as an important part of the national character. In the case study at hand the actor groups, scientists and affected actors were basically promoting two different frames where the first focused on structural adjustments and the latter on direct effects on rural communities. Whereas the scientific frame was focused on long-term impacts and risk assessments, the coverage of affected communities had much more of an emotional tone. This was so especially when individual farmers and their struggles were being portrayed. This means that even though the scientific frame had a strong impact in terms of status and authority, the affected actors' frame was equally powerful on an emotional level in relating to fundamental values such as culture, identity and solidarity. The cultural framing of measures to cope with the crisis might then account for why no major policy revisions in terms of what Boin et al. (2008) refer to as paradigm shifts, involving the altering of fundamental normative values, were thoroughly discussed in the coverage. Rather, the political framing connected to measures was rather focused on technical aspects and not the long-term implications of irrigation agriculture in a drought-prone area like the Murray–Darling Basin. This argument leads to the third proposition in relation to responsibility framing of 'climate change induced' crises.

4.3. Proposition three: Affected actors with strong cultural, economic and societal support will further limit political actors' framing options in terms of measures aimed at curbing the crisis

In summary, this paper has argued for research on crisis communication to take external (outside the media coverage) as well as internal (inside the media coverage) factors into account when examining responsibility frames in connection with compounded crises. In relation to the recommendations provided by Boin et al. (2005, p. 70), stating that successful meaning making requires the ability to communicate 'a persuasive story line that explains what happened, why it had to be that way, what its repercussions are, how it can be resolved, who can be relied upon, and who is to blame', the article at hand demonstrates how these storylines are constantly 'interrupted' by other actors. As illustrated in this article, the weight given to each actor group depends on the issue at hand, where different groups dominated the frames related to severity, causes and appropriate measures respectively. Together, this means that political actors' own storylines will be mediated and finally understood in the light of these other actors' framing. The dynamics of this framing contest will probably look different in various

cultural settings. In order to further develop the propositions above, additional studies will be needed.

Notes

1. It should thus be noted that, for example, political scientists Rosenthal et al. (2001, p. 20) open up a more dynamic approach to crisis aftermaths, proposing that 'Crises mark the transition from one stable pattern into one of many possible alternative futures. Actions taken during the crisis process become defining elements for the (temporary) resolution of that crisis, but at the same time, they become steps towards the creation of the next crisis.'

2. *The Australian* reported that 'Dr Nelson yesterday denied that he had rejected a link to climate change.' 'That is not what I said', he told ABC Radio in Adelaide. But in an interview with ABC presenter Tony Jones on Monday night's *Lateline* programme, Dr Nelson was asked explicitly whether he accepted that the Murray crisis was related to climate change. Dr Nelson replied initially, 'No, I do not' (ABC Radio, 4 September 2008).

3. Cubbie Station is a cotton farm in southern Queensland and is Australia's biggest irrigator, which has long been accused of taking too much water, in doing so denying farmers downstream water (ABC, 24 February 2004, www.abc.net.au/7.30/content/2004/s1052459.htm). In general, Australian cotton is mostly (82.5 per cent) grown under irrigation. 'From the growth of the first crop in 1961–62 near Wee Waa in the Namoi Valley cotton production has expanded rapidly to become one of Australia's major agricultural industries. It now makes a major contribution to the economies of the growing areas and to the Australian economy as a whole', www.mdbc.gov.au/subs/eResource_book/chapter3/p4.htm).

4. The connection between water management and climate change was justified by the fact that Minister Penny Wong was the minister for climate change *and* water.

5. The Coorong Wetlands are one of the most important wetlands in Australia. The wetland consists of ocean beach, the mouth of the Murray River, lakes and estuaries. This combination provides a wide range of habitats that vary from freshwater to hypersaline and which are for the most part in a natural state. The wetlands around the Coorong (including

Lake Alexandrina and Lake Albert) cover 140,500 ha. The Coorong is a long, shallow lagoon more than 100 km in length that is separated from the Southern Ocean by a narrow sand dune peninsula. Lakes Alexandrina and Albert form the mouth of the Murray River and are comprised of fresh to saline waters. The Coorong's fragile ecology depends on getting a mix of fresh water from the Murray River and sea water from the ocean.

References

Andreadis, E. and Smith, J., 2007. Beyond the oozone layer. *British Journalism Review*, 18(1). 50–56.

Beck, U., 2002. The terrorist threat: world risk society revisited. *Theory, Culture and Society*, 19(4). 3–55.

Beck, U., 2005. Freedom for technology: a call for a second separation of powers. *Dissent*, 42(4). 503–507.

Beck, U. and Lau, C., 2005. Second modernity as a research agenda: theoretical and empirical explorations in the 'meta-change' of modern society. *The British Journal of Sociology*, 56(4). 526–557.

Berglez, P., 2008. What is global journalism? *Journalism Studies*, 9(6). 845–858.

Boin, A., 't Hart, P., Stern, E. and Sundelius, B., 2005. *The Politics of Crisis Management: Public Leadership Under Pressure.* Cambridge University Press, New York, NY.

Boin, A., McConnell, A. and 't Hart, P., 2008. *Governing After Crisis: The Politics of Investigation, Accountability and Learning.* Cambridge University Press, Cambridge, UK.

Boin, A., McConnell, A. and 't Hart, P., 2009. Crisis exploitation: political and policy impacts of framing contests. *Journal of European Public Policy*, 16(1). 81–106.

Botterill, C. L., 2003. Uncertain climate: the recent history of drought policy in Australia. *Australian Journal of Politics and History*, 49(1). 61–74.

Brändström, A. and Kuipers, S., 2003. From 'normal incidents' to 'political crises': understanding the selective politicization of policy failures. *Government and Opposition*, 38(3). 279–305.

Brändström, A., Kuipers, S. and Daléus, P., 2008. The politics of tsunami responses: comparing patterns of blame management in scandinavia. *Governing after Crisis: The Politics of Investigation, Accountability and Learning*, A. Boin, A. McConnell and P. 't Hart. Cambridge University Press, Cambridge.

Buus, S. and Olsson, E.-K., 2006. The SARS crisis: was anybody responsible? *Journal of Contingencies and Crisis Management*, 14(2). 71–81.

Carvalho, A. and Burgess, J., 2005. Cultural circuits of climate change in UK broadsheet newspapers, 1985–2003. *Risk Analysis*, 25(6). 1457–1469.

Coombs, W. T., 1998. An analytical framework for crisis situations: better responses from a better understanding of the situation. *Journal of Public Relations Research* 10(3). 177–191.

Coombs, W. T., 2007. Attribution theory as a guide for post-crisis communication research. *Public Relations Review*, 33. 135–139.

Coombs, W. T. and Holladay, S. J., 2002. Helping crisis managers protect reputational assets: initial tests of the situational crisis communication theory. *Management Communication Quarterly*, 6(2). 165–186.

Cox, R., 2007. Crisis disciplines: does environmental communication have an ethical duty? *Environmental Communication*, 1(1). 5–20.

Dear, P., 2006. *The Intelligibility of Nature.* University of Chicago Press, Chicago, IL.

De Vries, M. S., 2004. Framing crises: response patterns to explosions in fireworks factories. *Administration and Society*, 36(5). 594–614.

Edelman, M., 1988. *Constructing the Political Spectacle.* University of Chicago Press, Chicago, IL.

Entman, R. M., 1993. Framing: toward clarification of a fractured paradigm. *Journal of Communication*, 43(4). 51–58.

Entman, R. M., 2003. Cascading activation: contesting the White House's frame after 9/11. *Political Communication*, 20(4). 415–432.

Fallows, J. M., 1996. *Breaking the News: How the Media Undermine American Democracy.* Pantheon Books, New York, NY.

Gamson, W., 1992. *Talking Politics.* Cambridge University Press, Cambridge, UK.

Gamson, W. A., 2004. Bystanders, public opinion and the media. *The Blackwell Companion to Social Movements*, D. A. Snow, S. A. Soule and H. Kriesi (eds). Blackwell, Oxford.

Gamson, W. A. and Stuart, D., 1992. Media discourse as a symbolic contest: the bomb in political cartoons. *Sociological Forum*, 7(1). 1573–7861.

Gerhards, J. and Rucht, D., 1992. Mesomobilization: organizing and farming in two protest campaigns in West Germany. *American Journal of Sociology*, 98(3). 555–596.

Goffman, E., 1974. *Frame Analysis: An Essay on the Organization of Experience.* Northeastern University Press, Boston, MA.

Goffman, E., 1981. A reply to Denzin and Keller. *Contemporary Sociology*, 10(1). 60–68.

Graber, D., 1988. *Processing the News: How People Tame the Information Tide*. Longman, New York, NY.

Graber, D., 1993. *Mass Media and American politics*. CQ Press, Washington, DC.

Gurevitch, M. and Levy, M. R., 1985. Introduction. *Mass Communication Yearbook*, Vol. 5, M. Gurevitch and M. R. Levy (eds). Sage, Beverly Hills, CA. 11–22.

Hallahan, K., 1999. Seven models of framing: implications for public relations. *Journal of Public Relations Research*, 11(3). 205–242.

Ihlen, O. and Nitz, M., 2008. Framing contest in environmental disputes: paying attention to media and cultural master frames. *International Journal of Strategic Communication*, 2(1). 1–18.

Iyengar, S., 1991. *Is Anyone Responsible? How Television Frames Political Issues*. University of Chicago Press, Chicago, IL.

Jamieson, K. H., 2001. *Everything You Think You Know About Politics... And Why You're Wrong*. Basic Books, New York, NY.

Krosnick, J., Visser, P. and Holbrook, A., 1998. American opinion on global warming: the impact of the Fall 1997 Debate. *Resources*, 133. 5–9.

Marcus, A. A. and Goodman, R. S., 1991. Victims and shareholders: the dilemma of presenting corporate policy during crisis. *Academy of Management Journal*, 34(2). 281–305.

Massey, J. E., 2001. Managing organizational legitimacy: communication strategies for organizations in crisis. *Journal of Business Communication*, 38(2). 153–182.

McComas, K. and Shanahan, J., 1999. Telling stories about global climate change: measuring the impact of narratives on issue cycles. *Communication Research*, 26(1). 30–57.

McLeod, J. M., Kosicki, G. M. and McLeod, D. M., 1994. The expanding boundaries of political communication effects. *Media Effects*, J. Bryant and D. Zillman (eds). Erlbaum, Hillsdale, NJ. 123–162.

Norris, P., Kern, M. and Just, M. (eds), 2003. *Framing Terrorism: The News Media, the Government and the Public*. Routledge, New York and London.

Olsson, E.-K. and Paglia, E., 2008. Global problem – national accountability: framing accountability in the Australian context of climate change, communicating climate change. *Journal of Contingencies and Crisis Management*, 16(2). 70–79.

Papacharissi, Z. and de Fatima Oliveira, M., 2008. News frames terrorism: a comparative analysis of frames employed in terrorism coverage in US and UK newspapers. *The International Journal of Press/Politics*, 13(1). 52–74.

Porfiriev, B., 2000. Preparing for creeping crises: the case of the Samara region. *Journal of Contingencies and Crisis Management*, 8(4). 218–222.

Rosenthal, U., Boin, A. and 't Hart, P., 2001. The changing world of crises and crisis management. *Managing Crises: Threats, Dilemmas and Opportunities*, U. Rosenthal, A. Boin and L. Comfort (eds). Charles C. Thomas, Springfield, IL.

Seeger, M. W., Sellnow, T. L. and Ulmer, R. R., 2003. *Communication and Organizational Crisis*. Praeger, Westport, CT.

Semetko, H. A. and Valkenburg, P. M., 2000. Framing European politics: a content analysis of press and television news. *Journal of Communication*, 50(2). 93–109.

Shih, T.-J., Wijaya, R. and Brossard, D., 2008. Media coverage of public health epidemics: linking framing and issue attention cycle toward an integrated theory of print news coverage of epidemics. *Mass Communication and Society*, 11(2). 141–160.

Simonson, P., 1999. Mediated sources of public confidence: Lazarsfeld and Merton revisited. *Journal of Communication*, 49(2). 109–122.

Siomkos, G. and Shrivastava, P., 1993. Responding to product liability crises. *Long Range Planning*, 26(5). 72–79.

't Hart, P., 1993. Symbols, rituals and power: the lost dimension of crisis management. *Journal of Contingencies and Crisis Management*, 1(1). 36–50.

't Hart, P. and Boin, A., 2001. Between crisis and normalcy: the long shadow of post-crisis politics. *Managing Crises: Threats, Dilemmas and Opportunities*, U. Rosenthal, A. Boin and L. Comfort (eds). Charles C. Thomas, Springfield, IL.

Ungar, S., 1992. The rise and (relative) decline of global warming as a social problem. *Sociological Quarterly*, 33(4). 483–501.

Ungar, S., 2008. Global bird flu communication: hot crisis and media reassurance. *Science Communication*, 29(4). 472–497.

Weingart, P., Engels, A. and Pansegrau, P., 2000. Risks of communication: discourses on climate change in science, politics, and the mass media. *Public Understanding of Science*, 9(3). 261–283.

West, B. and Smith, P., 1996. Drought, discourse, and Durkheim: a research note. *Journal of Sociology*, 32(1). 93–102.

Wolfsfeld, G., 1998. Promoting peace through the news media. Some initial lessons from the Oslo peace process. *Media, Ritual and Identity*, T. Liebes and J. Curran (eds). Routledge, London.

For Product Safety Concerns and Information please contact our EU
representative GPSR@taylorandfrancis.com Taylor & Francis Verlag GmbH,
Kaufingerstraße 24, 80331 München, Germany

Printed and bound by CPI Group (UK) Ltd, Croydon, CR0 4YY
11/05/2025
01866827-0001